FINANCIAL FANTASY

Your Life, Your Choices

A R Arnold

AUTHOR'S NOTE

Thank you for picking up *Financial Fantasy*. This book was created with the goal of making financial literacy accessible and engaging for everyone. Whether you're just beginning to explore personal finance or looking for a fresh perspective on money management, this book offers simple, easy-to-understand examples to help you navigate the world of finance.

The content is designed for a general audience, with concepts and scenarios that can apply to readers from all walks of life, regardless of where you live. While many of the financial principles discussed here - such as budgeting, saving, and investing - are universal, some scenarios may include examples that are more specific to certain countries, such as superannuation top-ups, tax advantages, or retirement savings plans. These examples are intended to provide a general understanding of the concepts, but may not directly align with the financial systems in every country. I have also used dollars and cents for the currency.

If you would like a version of this book tailored to the financial rules, benefits, and practices specific to your country, I welcome your feedback. Please feel free to reach out to me at info@themanfromuncool.com. I'll consider your request, and if there's enough interest, I will create a customized edition for your region.

Remember, financial literacy is a lifelong journey. This book is just the beginning, and I hope it helps set you on a path toward making confident, informed decisions about your money. Whether you're taking the first step or refining your financial strategy, I'm honored to be part of your journey.

Thank you again for reading, and I wish you all the best for your financial future.

With gratitude,

A.R. Arnold

Author

To Megan, who loves her budgeting spreadsheets and knowing where every cent is coming from and going to.

The best time to plant a tree was 20 years ago. The second best time is now.

CHINESE PROVERB

Introduction to Your Financial Fantasy Journey

This is no ordinary book.

Financial Fantasy is a unique adventure where every decision you make shapes your financial future. Think of this as part storybook, part personal finance guide, and part game, all designed to teach you the art of managing money while keeping things fun and engaging.

What Is This Book About?

Life is full of financial choices. From getting your first pay to buying a home, managing investments, and planning for retirement, each decision comes with opportunities, risks, and consequences. This book puts you in the driver's seat of your own financial story.

You'll start your journey as a teenager, navigating your first experiences with money, and follow through every stage of life, from early adulthood to retirement. Along the way, you'll encounter challenges, surprises, and milestones, just like in real life.

But here's the twist: you decide what happens next. Every chapter presents scenarios where you must choose a path. Should you save your money or spend it? Rent or buy a home? Take a financial risk or play it safe? Your choices lead to different outcomes, teaching you valuable lessons about money management, goal setting, and long-term planning.

How It Works

This book follows a "choose-your-own-adventure" format. Here's how to play:

1. **Start at Chapter One:** Begin your journey as a teenager. Read the scenario and the choices available to you.

2. **Make a Decision:** Each choice will guide you to a specific page. Turn to that page to see the consequences of your decision.

3. **Experience the Results:** Your decisions will shape your financial journey. Some choices lead to rewards, others to challenges, but every path teaches you something valuable. You will also receive or lose points depending on your decision so think carefully about the decisions you make.

4. Random Events: Life is unpredictable, so at certain points, you'll encounter chance-based scenarios. Toss a coin or use the book's random options to determine the outcome, just like real-life luck!

What You'll Learn

This isn't just a story, it's a hands-on way to learn the essentials of personal finance. Along the way, you'll explore key financial concepts, including:

- **Saving and Budgeting**: Learn how to manage your money wisely and plan for the future.

- **Compound Interest**: Discover how your money can grow exponentially over time.

- **Investing**: Understand the risks and rewards of different investment options.

- **Debt Management**: See how borrowing money impacts your financial health.

- **Tax Planning**: Learn to navigate taxes and make the most of your income.

- **Retirement and Legacy**: Prepare for your golden years and plan what you'll leave behind.

Keep Score

For each decision you make, you will have points awarded to you or taken from you. Keep score of your points so you can determine at the end of the book, how well you have you done and how wealthy you are!

By the end of the book, you'll have experienced the highs and lows of managing finances in a safe, interactive way. And, most importantly, you'll come away with the knowledge and confidence to tackle your real-life financial goals.

What This Book Hopes to Achieve

Money doesn't have to be intimidating or boring. Through storytelling and gameplay, this book aims to:

- **Make Finance Fun**: By putting financial decisions in a relatable, story-driven context, we hope to show that managing money can be as exciting as any adventure.

- **Build Confidence**: Through trial and error in a risk-free environment, you'll gain a better understanding of how to make smart financial choices in real life.

- **Encourage Reflection**: By seeing the long-term impact of your decisions, you'll learn the importance of thinking ahead and considering the bigger picture.

- **Empower You**: Whether you're just starting your financial journey or looking for fresh perspectives, this book is here to guide and inspire you.

Your Adventure Awaits

So, are you ready to take control of your financial future? Each choice you make will lead to new discoveries, challenges, and rewards. You might make some mistakes along the way, just like in real life, but every decision is a chance to learn.

This is your chance to explore financial life in a safe, playful, and insightful way.

So, take a breath, grab a pencil and piece of paper to keep score, then turn the page and begin your financial fantasy. The journey starts now, and the possibilities are endless.

All About Money

Before we get into it, let's take a moment to think about money itself.

Money, in its simplest form, is a tool, one that allows us to exchange value, acquire things, and achieve our goals. But far too often, we view money as something outside of ourselves, something that defines our worth or dictates our happiness. We think of it as either a source of power or something to be feared, but in reality, money is neither inherently good nor bad. It's simply a tool, much like a hammer or a wrench. It's not the tool that's problematic, but how we choose to wield it.

When we approach money with purpose, it can help us build the life we want. Imagine money as a bridge that connects you to opportunity, a safety net when things go wrong, and a megaphone that amplifies your values and what you stand for. It's the freedom to choose how you want to live, to invest in experiences, education, health, and even in causes that matter to you. With purpose, money can fuel your passions and drive, creating the space to do what you love and make a meaningful impact on the world around you.

The challenge, however, is that we're not often

taught how to use this tool. Many of us grow up without proper financial education. We don't learn how to manage money effectively, how to set healthy financial goals, or how to balance the short-term pleasures of spending with the long-term rewards of saving and investing. Instead, we learn through trial and error, often making mistakes along the way. These mistakes can feel like failures, and the financial world can become a place filled with stress, confusion, and even shame.

It's easy to compare ourselves to others, especially in a world that constantly shows us images of people who seem to have it all. Social media, advertising, and societal expectations often push us to strive for more, to want bigger homes, faster cars, and extravagant vacations. But the truth is, we never truly know the full story behind someone else's financial situation. The comparisons are often shallow, and they distract us from defining our own values and goals. We can get caught up in a cycle of wanting more, accumulating debt, and experiencing financial stress without ever pausing to ask ourselves: What do we actually want from money? What does financial success look like for us?

The silence around money often exacerbates this

problem. Money is a taboo topic for many, and talking about it openly can feel uncomfortable or even shameful. But it doesn't have to be that way. Financial health is just as important as physical and mental health, and it deserves to be approached with the same level of care and intention.

This book is here to change that narrative. It's here to guide you through the maze of financial decision-making and empower you to take control of your relationship with money. We'll break down the barriers of stress and confusion, helping you understand the basics of budgeting, saving, investing, and making money work for you. Together, we'll rewrite the script on money, so it becomes a tool that serves you and helps you live with purpose, confidence, and clarity.

By the end of this journey, you'll have a deeper understanding of how money can be used as a force for good in your life, enabling you to live the life you truly want - without fear, shame, or unnecessary stress. It's time to stop letting money control you and start taking charge of it, because when you understand how to use money with intention, the possibilities are endless.

Financial Fantasy Journey: The First Chapter of Life

You sit at the kitchen table, nervously drumming your fingers on your phone. Tomorrow is a big day, your very first shift at your new job. It's just a casual role at the local café, but it feels monumental. The thought of earning your own money is exciting, but also a little intimidating. What if you spill coffee on a customer? Or forget someone's order? What if you're just... bad at it?

Bethany, your older sibling, walks in with her usual mix of nonchalance and sarcasm. She grabs a banana from the fruit bowl and eyes you with mild amusement.

"Why do you look like you're about to take an exam?" she asks, peeling the banana.

"I start my job tomorrow," you mumble.

Bethany raises an eyebrow. "Ah, the big leap into adulthood. Welcome to the world of sweat and minimum wage. Don't worry, it's not rocket science."

"Thanks for the support," you say, rolling your eyes.

"Seriously, though," Bethany says between bites, "just

don't forget to smile and double-check the order before you take it to the table. You'll survive."

She saunters out of the room, leaving you alone with your nerves and a faintly growing sense of determination.

Your family is as supportive as they come, even if they each show it differently. Your mum works long shifts as a nurse, always encouraging you to treat people kindly, no matter how busy things get. "Patience gets you far," she likes to say. Your dad, an accountant, has a knack for slipping financial advice into everyday conversations. The first thing he said when you told him about the job? "Don't forget: always pay yourself first. Put some of it into savings."

And then there's Bethany, your older sibling. She's loud, quick-witted, and just the right amount of annoying. But despite her teasing, Bethany's taught you a lot, like how to budget your weekly allowance so you don't blow it all at once. And last summer, when you accidentally broke her favourite mug, she didn't even tell Mum and Dad. That's Bethany: a blend of nemesis and occasional lifesaver.

As you sit there, lost in thought, Muffin, your family's

fluffy grey cat, leaps onto the table. She nudges your arm and purrs loudly, as if sensing your stress. You scratch behind her ears, and Muffin rewards you with a contented flop onto her back.

"You've got it easy," you mutter. "All you have to do is nap and eat."

Muffin blinks up at you, unimpressed by your plight, before resuming her quest for rubs. Somehow, her presence makes everything feel just a little less overwhelming.

Your phone buzzes, snapping you out of your thoughts. It's a message from Alex, your best friend since Year 3.

Alex: You ready for tomorrow? First shift!

You: Ready? No. Nervous? Yes. What if I mess up?

Alex: Relax, it's not brain surgery. Worst case? You accidentally serve someone a latte when they wanted a flat white. You'll live.

You laugh, feeling a bit lighter. Then Sam, another close friend, chimes in:

Sam: You'll be fine. Just stay calm and follow the system. Cafés are all about routine. You're good at that.

You smile at their messages. Alex and Sam have always been there for you, and you know they'll want to hear all about your first day, every awkward, caffeine-filled moment of it.

At dinner, your parents offer their usual mix of advice and encouragement. Mum reminds you to have a proper breakfast and keep hydrated. Dad talks about the importance of setting aside a portion of your earnings for savings. And Bethany, of course, has her own input.

"Don't forget to take a notebook," she says. "Write down the weirdest customer request. You'll thank me later."

Later that night, as you get ready for bed, you catch a glimpse of Muffin curled up on your desk chair. She stretches lazily, her tail flicking back and forth. Somehow, her calmness feels contagious. You climb into bed, thoughts of coffee orders and dishwashing spinning through your head, until exhaustion finally pulls you into sleep.

The next morning, you wake up to the smell of toast

and the sound of Bethany playing music too loudly in her room. Your dad hands you a packed lunch as you grab your bag, and your mum hugs you on her way out to work.

"Good luck," she says with a smile. "First jobs are about learning. You'll do great."

Bethany appears in the doorway, her usual smirk in place. "Don't break anything," she says. "Or do. Makes a better story."

As you step outside, the air feels crisp and full of possibility. Muffin watches from the window, tail swishing rhythmically as if to say, "You've got this." Taking a deep breath, you start walking toward the café, ready to begin the next chapter of your life. This is it! And, while you don't know what's ahead, you're ready to tackle it, one step at a time.

First Job, First Pay, First Choice

Age: 16

You start your first job - weekends at Café Junction. The pay's not huge, but that doesn't matter. You're earning your own money now. You wear your black apron like a badge of honour, even if it still smells faintly of toasted cheese and burnt coffee grounds.

Alex has been working at the petrol station down the road for a few months and meets you after your shift. "How was your first real day in the grind?" they ask, handing you a fizzy drink.

You shrug, smiling. "Kinda loved it."

That Friday, your first pay lands. $120. Your name's on the payslip and everything. It's a thrill. Your bank app lights up and so do your ideas. Will it be new sneakers, that concert next weekend, or takeout with your friends. You've never had this kind of freedom before.

But later that evening, your dad catches sight of your beaming face and says, "Feels good, doesn't it? Just remember, don't just work for money. Make it work for you."

You don't think much of it at first. But in bed that night, it echoes in your head.

You now face your first financial decision.

You open your banking app. The $120 is still there. Waiting. Shiny.

Do you:

> **1.** Spend the lot this weekend: go shopping, dinner with friends, book the concert ticket?
>
> → **Go to Page 67**
>
> **2.** Save half, spend half: you can go out, but maybe skip the shopping for now?
>
> → **Go to Page 32**

Invest in Your Grandchildren's Future

You and Riley sit at the dining table with two mugs of tea and a spreadsheet. "We've done more than enough for ourselves," you say. "Let's help them get ahead."

You open new investment accounts for your grandchild - a mix of index funds and education bonds. You don't give them the money directly, but set it aside to grow, ready to help with school fees, apprenticeships, or even a home deposit someday.

You also write a letter to be opened when they turn 18. Inside: your story, your financial lessons, and a wish for them to live boldly, wisely, and kindly.

Points: +10

Lesson: Intergenerational wealth isn't about giving money, it's about giving opportunity. Starting early, even with modest contributions, can mean thousands more by the time they need it. Combine this with wisdom, and you're passing down more than money, you're passing down *legacy*.

→ **Go to Page 139**

Stick to the Job

You stay put. It's safe. You take on more responsibility informally, get a small raise, and become "the go-to" person in your team.

You're comfortable but wonder if you missed a window to grow further. Five years later, your income has increased modestly but others who re-skilled have leapfrogged you.

Points: -5

Lesson: Stability is valuable but without growth, your income may plateau. While not every investment in education pays off, failing to adapt to changing industries can limit long-term opportunities.

→ **Go to Page 145**

Sell in Fear

You pull the plug. Sell everything. You get $465 back, which is $35 less than you started with. The relief is short-lived. Three weeks later, the market rebounds, and your ETF is worth $510. You missed the recovery. A little research tells you this kind of volatility is normal. What felt like a smart escape was really a panic move.

Points: –5

Lesson: The stock market has ups and downs. Selling during a dip means you *lock in* a loss. Historically, markets recover over time. For example:

- Over any 10-year period in the S&P 500 (a major US index), there's been a 94% chance of positive returns.

- Over 20 years? 100% of periods have shown growth, averaging around 8–10% annually, even accounting for recessions.

(Source: Morningstar, Vanguard)

Investing is a long game. Patience pays.

→ **Go to Page 42**

Push Through

You decide to press on. "I've made it this far. I'll rest when I'm retired."

You resume work, but it's not the same. The stress builds again. You skip the gym, eat takeaway, sleep poorly. Riley notices. "You're not yourself."

By 58, you're diagnosed with high blood pressure and need medication. It's manageable, but it shakes you. You realise you've been ignoring signs. You start making changes but only after a serious scare.

You still retire at 65 with a strong super balance, but your energy isn't what it could've been.

Points: −5

Lesson: Delaying care or ignoring your body can undermine the life you've worked so hard to build. Pushing through may maximise dollars - but **at what cost**? Money is replaceable. Time and health aren't.

→ **Go to Page 101**

Random Life Event: Tax Time Windfall

Your accountant (or app) lodges your return. Thanks to your careful record-keeping, work expenses, and a bit of salary sacrificing, you get a $2,100 tax refund. Riley gets $1,200.

You smile. "What should we do with it?"

How do you spend the unexpected refund?

1. Use it all on a spontaneous luxury weekend escape.
   → **Go to Page 184**
2. Put it toward investments or superannuation.
   → **Go to Page 126**
3. Split it-half for fun, half for future.
   → **Go to Page 33**

Save for Another Big Life Goal

You open a new savings account and label it "Dreams". You and Riley agree to put away $400/month for a mix of maybe things like maybe travel, maybe a future baby, or maybe a business idea. It's flexible, and it keeps you dreaming. But your investments and super don't grow as fast.

Points: +5

Lesson: Saving for short-term goals is important too. Not all money needs to be locked up in super or the stock market. Just make sure your long-term needs aren't ignored in the process.

→ **Go to Page 125**

Congratulations on Deciding to Budget!

Well done! Deciding to start budgeting is a huge step toward taking control of your money. It means you're ready to plan how to use your income wisely, whether it's from a part-time job, allowance, or the occasional odd job. Budgeting isn't about saying no to fun, it's about making sure your money goes to the things that matter most to you.

Now that you're ready, let's break down exactly how to create and stick to a budget that works for you.

How to Split Up Your Money

One of the easiest ways to budget is by dividing your income into categories, so you always know where your money is going. Here's a simple and effective way to do it:

1. 50% - Needs and Essentials

This is for things you absolutely need. If you don't have many financial responsibilities right now, this category might be small. But if you're covering things like school supplies, bus fares, or chipping in at home, make sure you plan for these first.

2. 30% - Fun and Wants

This is your "treat yourself" category! Use this money for snacks, outings with friends, gaming, or that new gadget you've been eyeing. Enjoy it guilt-free but remember to stay within the 30% limit.

3. 20% - Savings

This is the money you set aside for the future. Maybe you're saving for a bigger goal like a new bike, a concert ticket, or a long-term emergency fund. Treat this category like it's non-negotiable. Pay yourself first, and watch your savings grow!

Step-by-Step Budgeting Plan

Here's how to start budgeting today:

1. **Know Your Income**
   Start by figuring out how much money you have coming in weekly or monthly. For example, if you earn $100 a week, that's your total budget to work with.

2. **Divide Your Money**
   Split your income using the 50/30/20 rule. If you're earning $100 a week, your budget

might look like this:
- $50 for needs and essentials
- $30 for fun and wants
- $20 for savings

3. **Set a Goal for Savings**
Write down what you're saving for and how much you'll need. For example:
- New headphones: $80 → Save $20 a week for 4 weeks.
- A concert ticket: $120 → Save $20 a week for 6 weeks. Having a goal makes saving more exciting!

4. **Track Your Spending**
Keep a record of where your money goes. Use a notebook, an app, or even the notes on your phone. This will help you see if you're staying within your budget.

5. **Review and Adjust**
Check your progress every week or two. If you're spending too much on fun, adjust by cutting back slightly. If you have extra money left over, you can add it to savings or enjoy a small treat.

Tips for Budgeting Success

- **Use Cash or Prepaid Cards:** If you find it hard to stick to your budget, use cash or a prepaid card. When the money's gone, it's gone!

- **Start a Savings Account:** Open a bank account to keep your savings safe and out of sight (so you're not tempted to spend it).

- **Set a Goal:** Saving is easier when you know what you're working toward. Write down your goals and how much you need to save each week to reach them.

- **Learn from Mistakes:** If you overspend one week, don't stress, just adjust for the next week. Budgeting is all about progress, not perfection.

You're On Your Way!

By deciding to budget, you've taken a big step toward financial independence. Whether you're saving for something exciting, making sure you have enough for everyday needs, or just learning how to manage money, budgeting is the foundation for success. Stick with it, and you'll soon see how powerful it can be. Keep going. You've got this!

Points: +10

→ **Go to Page 57**

Hold Through the Dip

You grit your teeth and decide to wait. "This is for the long-term," you remind yourself. You stop checking the app daily. A month later, the market rebounds, and your investment not only recovers but grows to $510. You feel proud, not because of the money, but because you didn't panic. Riley high-fives you. "Told you."

Points: +5

Lesson: Market dips are normal. In fact, they're expected. The key is to think long-term. By staying in the market, you let time and compound growth work in your favour. Historically, patient investors come out ahead.

→ **Go to Page 42**

Delay Your Plans for a Child Until You've Saved More or Paid Off More Debt

You and Riley talk long into the night. After discussing your finances, you both realize that while you're excited about the prospect of becoming parents, the current financial strain may make things difficult. Your debt, while manageable, still needs attention, and you both agree that it might be better to wait a few years to ensure you're financially stable before bringing a child into the world. You decide to focus on paying off your debts and building a larger emergency fund in the meantime.

Although the delay is disappointing, you both feel confident that it's the right decision. You spend the next two years paying off your student loans and building a more substantial financial cushion. When the time finally comes to start your family, you're in a much stronger financial position, and you feel ready to face the challenges of parenthood.

Points: -5

Lesson: Delaying starting a family to pay off debt and save more can be a wise decision, but it comes with the risk of lost time. While the delay provides financial security, it's important to balance preparation with living in the present and making the most of the time you have.

→ **Go to Page 97**

Spend Freely

You tell yourself you'll save later. You deserve this new lifestyle, after all. You upgrade your wardrobe, eat out more, and take a weekend trip to the coast. The money goes fast. Within a few months, you realise you've got nothing left. When your car needs a service, you put it on a credit card. It starts to add up.

Points: -10

Lesson: Lifestyle creep is real. The more you earn, the more you're tempted to spend. Without a plan, it all disappears.

→ **Go to Page 175**

Random Life Event: Unexpected Inheritance

Riley's distant uncle passes away, and to everyone's surprise, Riley is left **$10,000**. "I wasn't that close to him," they say, "but I want to use it wisely."

They ask for your input.

What do you decide to do with the money together?

1. Blow it on a holiday, new furniture, and a home entertainment system.
   → **Go to Page 152**
2. Use half to upgrade your lifestyle and save the rest for future goals.
   → **Go to Page 185**
3. Invest the entire amount toward your house deposit or long-term investments.
   → **Go to page 172**

Save a Little

You decide to stash $60 into a savings account. The rest? Enough for dinner out and a movie with your friends. On Sunday, your phone charger dies but this time, it's no big deal. You buy a replacement with your own money. You feel... prepared. Grown-up.

Points: +10

Lesson: Saving even a little gives you freedom later. It's not about having less fun, it's about having fewer problems.

→ **Go to Page 132**

Split the Difference

You and Riley agree to keep things balanced. "We should enjoy some of it," they say, "but let's be smart too."

You take $1,000 for a weekend away - nothing too lavish, just a few nights at a country cottage, hiking, relaxing, and treating yourselves. The other $1,100 goes into savings and investments. It's the perfect middle ground.

You return feeling great and proud of yourself. You had your fun and didn't lose sight of your bigger goals.

Points: +5

Lesson: Moderation can be powerful. You enjoy your money now, *and* set yourself up for later. It's proof that good financial habits don't have to be all-or-nothing. Life is for living, not just saving.

→ **Go to Page 135**

Create a Joint Account for Shared Expenses

You and Riley agree to keep your individual accounts but also set up a shared account for rent, bills, groceries, and joint goals. You each contribute a percentage based on income, which feels fair. There are no more awkward conversations about who owes what. You even start saving together for a future trip to Japan.

Points: +10

Lesson: Joint accounts for shared costs can improve financial transparency and reduce conflict, especially when income is uneven. It helps create structure without giving up independence.

→ **Go to Page 38**

The Gap Year Gamble

You travel and work bar shifts across hostels and cafes. You meet people from around the world and experience freedom. You also spend more than you thought.

By the time you return, your savings are low. Riley's halfway through their course. You feel enriched emotionally but financially, you're behind.

Points: -5

Lesson: Time is valuable. A break can be worth it, but comes at a cost. Always balance personal growth with financial impact.

→ **Go to Page 85**

Insurance First

You both get life insurance policies and income protection - just in case. It's not glamorous, and paying monthly premiums stings a bit. But it gives you peace of mind. If something happened to one of you, the other could stay afloat.

A year later, a friend unexpectedly loses their partner. The grief is unimaginable, and without insurance, the financial stress is overwhelming. You feel lucky, and more than a little relieved.

Points: +10

Lesson: Insurance is about *risk management*. Life insurance can protect your family from financial ruin. Income protection covers your salary if you can't work due to illness or injury. It's money you hope to never use but *must* have.

→ **Go to Page 176**

Put It on a Credit Card

The quote comes in and your heart sinks. $7,200. You don't have that kind of cash on hand, and you didn't add roof coverage to your insurance - an oversight from when you tried to save on premiums.

With no other choice, you put the bill on your credit card. The limit is high enough to cover it, but the interest is punishing at 19.99%. You plan to pay it off quickly, but then the car needs new tyres, school fees come due, and you fall behind.

Six months later, you're still carrying a $6,000 balance, and the stress is building. You and Riley agree to cut back hard. There will be no holidays, no takeaways, no new anything. Slowly, painfully, the debt shrinks.

Points: -10

Lesson: Credit cards are useful *tools*, not safety nets. Without a plan for major expenses, you risk falling into high-interest debt that erodes financial stability. Always plan for the unexpected, and double-check your insurance policies.

→ **Go to Page 119**

** Mini Concept: Budgeting as a Couple **

Whether you share everything or just expenses, a shared budget is your roadmap. Use the 50/30/20 rule as a guide:

- 50% needs (rent, bills, groceries)
- 30% wants (dining out, hobbies, travel)
- 20% savings (emergency fund, investments, house fund)

Budgeting isn't about restriction, it's about intention.

Success with Detailed Budgeting

Setting up a detailed budget actually takes a bit of time and commitment. You and Riley sit down at the kitchen table with notebooks, receipts, bank statements, and a shared goal in mind. Muffin, your ever-curious cat, jumps up on the table to supervise, batting at the calculator while Riley rolls their eyes and shoos her away. "This might actually be fun," they joke. You're not convinced - yet.

Creating the Budget

The first step is figuring out where your money is going. You both start listing out expenses: rent, groceries, phone bills, and that seemingly innocent habit of grabbing coffee on the way to work. When Riley tallies up the total, the numbers are eye-opening. "I didn't realise we were spending this much on takeaway," you admit, glancing at a stack of receipts from your favourite pizza place.

Together, you set some goals. The trip to Japan tops the list, followed by smaller, more immediate ones, like setting aside money for a house deposit. You decide to track every dollar for a month, splitting expenses into categories and setting limits for each one.

The Weekly Check-In

Over the next few weeks, budgeting becomes a regular part of your routine. Every Sunday evening, you and Riley sit down with cups of tea to review your progress. The first week is rough. You both overspend on entertainment, and Riley discovers they forgot to account for their gym membership. "It's a learning curve," they says, adding the expense to the spreadsheet.

By the third week, things start to click. You find yourselves more conscious of your spending, opting to cook at home instead of ordering out and making coffee at home instead of grabbing it on the go. You're both surprised at how quickly the savings start to add up. "This feels... kind of empowering," you admit during one of your Sunday check-ins. Riley smiles. "Told you it might be fun."

Building Momentum

As the months go by, budgeting becomes second nature. The Japan fund grows steadily, and you've even managed to save enough for a weekend getaway as a reward for sticking to the plan. One evening, as you're planning your upcoming trip, Riley brings up the idea of moving in together. "We're already working so well as a team," they say, looking at you hopefully. It's a big step, but it feels like the natural next one.

The thought of shared rent and splitting bills excites both of you. You decide to add "apartment savings" as a new category in your budget, setting a clear timeline for when you'd like to make it happen. It's amazing how much more confident you feel about the future, knowing you've got a system that works.

The Confidence of Preparation

Budgeting together hasn't just helped you save money, it's strengthened your relationship. You've learned to communicate better, compromise, and support each other's goals. And it's not just about the numbers; it's about the shared vision of a future you're building together.

One evening, as you sit on the couch with Muffin curled up between you, Riley turns to you and says, "I think we're really good at this adulting thing." You laugh, but deep down, you agree. For the first time, you feel genuinely prepared for whatever life throws your way, confident in your habits and excited about what's to come.

→ **Go to Page 31**

Moving In Together, Budgeting as a Team, and Big Dreams

Age: 23

Things between you and Riley are going great. You've both been working for a couple of years now, getting more confident with money, careers, and what you want out of life. On a rainy Sunday afternoon, curled up on the couch with Muffin the cat snoozing between you, Riley says it out loud:

"Maybe it's time we moved in together."

You pause. It makes sense. You're already spending most nights at each other's places, and it could save money too. You run the numbers and realise you could cut rent and utilities almost in half by sharing. But you also know that financial habits can make or break relationships. Time for some planning.

Together, you make a spreadsheet. You list income, expenses, and savings goals. It's a mix of exciting and awkward because you're used to handling your money alone. Now, you'll be splitting groceries, rent, streaming subscriptions, and more.

You face your next big decision: how do you handle

your money together?

1. Create a joint account for shared expenses and agree on monthly contributions.
   → **Go to Page 34**
2. Keep everything separate and just split bills manually each month.
   → **Go to Page 156**
3. Combine all finances completely - it's easier to manage as one pool.
   → **Go to Page 138**

Budgeting Basics

You are saving but with social expectations and pressures, you are saving less than you really want. In fact, over the next few weeks, it's like the money burns a hole in your pocket. One Friday afternoon, your friends Alex and Sam invite you to the shopping centre. You tell yourself you're just tagging along, but when you see a new pair of sneakers that everyone says look awesome, it's hard to resist. A quick swipe of your card, and they're yours.

The next weekend, there's a party at a classmate's house, and everyone's chipping in for snacks and drinks. It's only $10 here, $15 there, but it adds up. On top of that, your phone charger breaks, so you have to grab a replacement, and don't even get started on that "quick" stop for lunch after sports practice. By the end of the month, your bank balance is almost back to where it started.

At first, it doesn't bother you. You had fun, and the sneakers were worth it but then, one rainy Sunday, you find yourself scrolling through your wishlist for new clothes. When you check your bank account, reality hits: there's barely enough left for your regular expenses. You sigh, thinking about how nice it would be to have a little extra set aside.

As you lie back on the couch, Muffin hops up beside you, curling into a ball on your chest. You scratch behind her ears, and the thought nags at you again: Maybe it's time to start saving again. Just a little. You make a mental note to do better next month, promising yourself you'll start putting a bit more of your pay aside but that month passes and you are still not getting ahead. You need help. You talk to your dad (he is an accountant after all) and tell him what has been happening and that you find it hard to stop spending when it gives you so much in return but that you don't want to see all your savings disappearing.

Your dad stops what he is doing. You have tapped into one of his great interests (aside from World War Two and footy – two things all dads seem to be interested in!).

Dad: I think what you need is a budget.

You: How will that help?

Dad: You simply put aside money for specific things. For example, you might put aside a specific amount or a percentage of your income for different things. Let's say you save 50% of your income, 40% of your income is for doing things with your friends, like going out to movies and parties etc, and the remaining 10% is for unexpected expenses but you save it if you can.

You: That sounds like a lot to save.

Dad: Well, that is just an example. You can pick whatever amount you want but the more the better. Trust me, your expenses get bigger the older you get so the more you can save now, the better.

You have a decision to make. What do you want to do?

1. **Try Budgeting**: You set aside a portion for essentials and some for fun.

   → **Go to page 22.**

2. **Skip Budgeting**: Keep spending without a plan, hoping things balance out.

   → **Go to page 95.**

Higher Risk, Higher Reward

You invest in a mix of ETFs and a small real estate trust. For a while, it grows rapidly but then, a market downturn shakes your confidence.

Thankfully, you didn't invest emotionally or reactively. You hold firm, and after a few years, your investments rebound and grow stronger.

Points: +5

Lesson: With the right risk tolerance, diversified investing can provide significant growth but you need patience and a long-term view.

→ **Go to Page 80**

Market Crash

It starts with a news headline:

"Global Economic Downturn Imminent: Markets React Sharply."

You log into your investment app and stare. Your portfolio has dropped 15% overnight. Tens of thousands have vanished, at least on paper. Riley looks over your shoulder and swears under their breath. "What do we do?"

You feel the urge to sell. To stop the bleeding. But you don't. You remember what you have learned. The small dip back then. How it bounced back. This is just bigger. You take a breath. Then you do the smartest thing you can: nothing.

Instead of panic, you revisit your plan. You rebalance your portfolio, ride out the storm, and lean into dollar-cost averaging - continuing to invest the same amount each month regardless of market performance. It's painful, yes. But you've been here before.

Six months later, the market begins to recover. Slowly, then faster. Within two years, your portfolio not only regains its losses, it grows beyond where it started.

Points: +10

Lesson: Market crashes are normal. Historically, the stock market recovers from every major downturn. Since 1900, the average bear market (a drop of 20% or more) has lasted about 14 months, but the average bull market has lasted 5–7 years.

Holding steady and sticking to your plan almost always beats trying to time the market.
Your wealth grows not because you avoided downturns but because you stayed invested through them.

→ **Go to Page 162**

Work with a Financial Adviser

You book a session with a licensed adviser. They help you project your retirement needs, optimise your super, set up a will, and advise on tax strategies. It feels like you've taken control of the next 20 years of your life.

You discover you're slightly behind on your retirement targets but with a few changes (including consolidating your super accounts and trimming some underperforming investments), you can catch up.

Points: +10

Lesson: Financial advisers aren't just for the wealthy, they're for the *prepared*. A good adviser can help maximise returns, reduce taxes, and reduce stress. Just be sure to choose one who is independent and fee-for-service.

→ **Go to Page 149**

A Smart Ceremony

You invite close family and friends to a beautiful garden ceremony. You skip the extras but keep the joy.

The day feels deeply personal and, best of all, you're not financially drained afterward. That night, you transfer your leftover wedding fund into a savings account labelled "For Our Home."

Points: +5

Lesson: A celebration doesn't have to cost a fortune. Financial freedom often comes from intentional choices.

→ **Go to Page 64**

Wedding Bells and Wallets

Age: 28

You and Riley are inseparable. Life together is good. You both have steady jobs now, and conversations turn to the future. One day, on a weekend trip to the coast, Riley proposes. You say yes, heart racing.

Suddenly, you're planning a wedding.

The spreadsheet quickly grows to include venue, dress, food, DJ, and more. Riley wants something intimate, while you secretly imagine a big bash. Your parents offer some support, but you'll need to cover most of it yourselves.

Meanwhile, you've also been eyeing homes online. The wedding budget starts to feel like a fork in the road.

Your Choice:

> 1. Spend big on your dream wedding and celebrate in style.
>   → **Go to Page 90**

> 2. Keep the wedding modest and save the rest for a home.
>   → **Go to Page 51**

Put It on a Credit Card

You don't have enough in savings, so you put the $2,800 on your credit card. You promise yourself you'll pay it off soon.

But after the baby arrives, life becomes a whirlwind of nappies, midnight feeds, formula, and bills. Your balance grows faster than you can pay it down.

Six months in, you're making minimum repayments, and interest is stacking up at around 19% per year. You feel stuck. The card, once your fallback, now feels like a burden.

Riley's supportive, but you both agree: you need a plan. You pause investments, reduce spending, and funnel everything toward debt. It takes discipline, but eventually, you claw your way out.

Points: -10

Lesson: Credit cards should *never* be your emergency fund. At 19% interest, that $2,800 could balloon to over $3,700 in 12 months if only minimum payments are made. Borrowing for emergencies can lock you into long-term financial stress.

→ **Go to Page 170**

Education Savings

You open a dedicated investment account and start contributing $250/month for school fees and future university costs. You choose a diversified portfolio with long-term growth in mind. It doesn't feel like much at first, but after five years, it grows to over $17,000.

Your child may not notice yet but future-you will.

Points: +10

Lesson: Starting early, even with small amounts, builds significant savings over time. Education costs can reach $60,000–$100,000+ per child across their schooling. Investing now avoids panic later.

→ **Go to Page 176**

Use Savings and Insurance

The rain hasn't even stopped before you're on the phone with your insurance provider. You'd taken out comprehensive coverage when you bought the house and opted for a reasonable excess. The inspection confirms the damage is covered although you'll need to pay $1,000 out of pocket.

You also dip into your home maintenance savings and emergency fund to cover the shortfall. It hurts a little, watching $6,200 vanish from your account, but you get the roof repaired immediately. Your home is secure again. You sleep soundly that night, listening to the rain, this time on the *outside* of the roof, not the inside.

Riley puts a reminder in your calendar: "Rebuild emergency fund."

You nod, but you're proud. The system worked. You planned for this.

Points: +10

Lesson: Planning ahead doesn't stop bad things from happening, it just makes them manageable. Home repairs are one of the most common and costly surprises. Insurance + savings = peace of mind.

→ **Go to Page 119**

Try a Micro-Credential

You find a 6-week online certificate for $700. It gives you a taste of the field - enough to build confidence and update your résumé. You network on LinkedIn and land some freelance side gigs.

Eventually, you decide to pursue further study but now with more certainty.

Points: +5

Lesson: Start small, test your interest, and build confidence. Not all learning has to be expensive. Micro-credentials and online courses are cost-effective stepping stones for career pivots, especially if you're unsure.

→ **Go to Page 145**

Young Love, New Habits, and Bigger Choices

Age: 18

Two years fly by.

You're in your final year of school. You've kept your café job, picked up a few extra shifts during holidays, and grown a small but steady savings account - if you chose wisely, that is.

Your friend, Riley, is now officially more than just a friend. You've been together for nearly a year, and while your dates are mostly casual such as picnics, cheap movie nights, or wandering bookstores, you wouldn't trade them for anything.

One Friday afternoon, after your shift, Riley's waiting outside with that look. "My car broke down again. Mechanic says it's the alternator... or the starter... or both. It's dead."

The bus system's unreliable. Riley's stressed. "I've got university interviews next month. Work. Everything. I can't afford a new car."

That night, you're at home thinking about it. You've saved up $1,200 over the last two years. It's the most you've ever had. You're proud of that number. You keep your savings in a high-interest account your dad helped you set up, so it's slowly been growing thanks to *compound interest*, where you earn interest on your interest, like money multiplying quietly in the background.

But now you wonder: should you use some of it to help Riley?

Here's the situation:

Riley needs $800 for a reliable used car. Their family can cover $400. They're short the other half.

They've never asked, but you know they're struggling.

Do you:

1. Lend Riley the $400: because that's what partners do.
   → **Go to Page 130**
2. Gift them the $400: you don't want money between you.
   → **Go to Page 59**
3. Say no: you've been saving for your future, and it's not your responsibility.
   → **Go to Page 75**

Gift the Money

Riley's speechless. They promise to pay you back, but you wave it off. "What are savings for, if not helping someone you love?" They get the car, and life rolls on. But over time, you feel the sting as your savings drop, and they don't quite treat the money like it mattered. It doesn't hurt your relationship, but you quietly realise you gave more than you could afford.

Points: -5

Lesson: Generosity is beautiful, but giving large amounts can hurt your financial future. Always assess whether you can *truly* afford to give.

→ **Go to Page 106**

Random Life Event: Major Home Repairs Needed

During a storm, your roof leaks badly. After inspections and quotes, the total bill comes to **$7,200**.

You:

1. Use savings and insurance to cover it with minimal stress.
   → **Go to Page 55**
2. Put it on your credit card and juggle repayments later.
   → **Go to Page 37**
3. Delay the repairs for six months while you save.
   → **Go to Page 108**

Preparing for the Future (Age 45)

Time is moving quickly. Your child is now a teenager, and the conversations around the dinner table shift to high school, career aspirations, and pocket money negotiations.

You and Riley are still working full-time, but you've started to think seriously about retirement. Should you begin scaling back and focusing on lifestyle, or continue to maximise earnings while you can?

Then, your aunt passes away, and you receive an unexpected inheritance. It's not a fortune but enough to make a difference.

Riley suggests using some of it to accelerate your retirement savings, while you wonder if investing it in property or shares might yield more in the long term.

Your Choice:

1. Add the inheritance to your superannuation.
   → **Go to Page 71**

2. Use it to invest in shares or property.
   → **Go to Page 47**

Withdraw a Higher Percentage for the First Few Years

You and Riley feel like you've earned the right to enjoy life now. After a long career, you're ready to dive into those travel adventures and experiences you've dreamed about. You decide to withdraw 6% per year for the first few years of your retirement, thinking that you'll enjoy these early years while you're still physically active and eager to explore the world.

In the first few years, everything feels great. You travel to exotic locations, buy a motorhome for road trips, and start ticking off items from your bucket list. You feel like you're making up for lost time, and every new adventure feels like a reward for your years of hard work.

But as the years pass, you start to notice something unsettling. Your investment portfolio, while still growing, isn't growing as quickly as you had hoped. The higher withdrawal rate is starting to take its toll. After a few years, you realize that you've been drawing down faster than anticipated, and while you've enjoyed every moment of it, you begin to feel a bit of concern.

You and Riley sit down with a financial advisor

to reassess. Together, you decide to lower your withdrawal rate to 4% for the remaining years of your retirement. The damage, however, is already done. You realize that, by the time you're in your 80s, your portfolio will likely run out faster than expected, even with the reduction in withdrawals.

Points: +5

Lesson: While it's tempting to spend more in the early years of retirement, withdrawing too much too quickly can result in financial insecurity later on. A higher withdrawal rate can limit the sustainability of your savings, so a cautious approach is always best for the long term.

→ **Go to Page 123**

Growing Wealth - Super, Tax, and the Long Game

Age: 29

Life is starting to feel more stable. You've settled into your home, you're earning more, and your confidence is growing, both at work and in your finances. Riley's been promoted, and you've found your rhythm in your new job. You even catch yourself enjoying budgeting sometimes.

One Saturday morning, over pancakes and coffee, Riley brings up something you've both avoided.

"We should probably talk about superannuation," they say. "And taxes. And all that... adult stuff."

You pull out your laptops and start digging into your superannuation accounts. You've both been contributing the default 11% from your employer, but you notice your balances aren't exactly thrilling. You read about voluntary contributions, which is money you can add yourself, which gets taxed at just 15%, instead of your regular income tax rate (which is probably over 30%).

You also find out about salary sacrificing - an arrangement where your employer sends some of your pre-tax income directly into super. It lowers your taxable income and helps grow your retirement fund.

At the same time, Riley stumbles across an article about capital gains tax. "So if we sell our shares one day and they've gone up in value, we have to pay tax on the profits?" they ask.

You nod slowly. "Seems like we've got more learning to do."

You come to a fork in the financial road.

With some room in your budget, you now have extra money to play with each month. Do you:

1. Focus on salary sacrificing into superannuation to maximise retirement savings and reduce your tax bill?
   → **Go to Page 100**
2. Keep investing in the stock market to try and grow your wealth more quickly?
   → **Go to Page 122**
3. Start saving for another big life goal like travel, a potential business, or even a baby?
   → **Go to Page 21**

Hit the Shops

You hit the shops Saturday morning. New sneakers? Tick. Burgers and bubble tea with your mates? Tick. Sunday rolls around, and you're broke. When your phone charger breaks, you find yourself staring at the cracked cable like it personally betrayed you. You ask your mum for a loan. She sighs. You feel a twinge of regret. That money was here and gone faster than a Snapchat.

Points: -10

Lesson: Spending everything feels great - for a day. But without savings, even small surprises become big problems.

→ **Go to Page 132**

Investing in Education

Age: 41

Scene Title: Back to School?

You're feeling the itch. Your job's stable, but there's a cap, and you know it. Lately, you've been eyeing a career shift: digital marketing, maybe project management. You stumble across a postgraduate certificate, costing $10,000 and taking 12 months part-time.

Riley raises an eyebrow. "It's a big investment... but if it leads to more income or happiness, maybe it's worth it?"

You do the maths. The new qualification could bump your salary from $85,000 to $100,000+ in two years. But it means juggling study, work, and family, not to mention spending money now without an immediate return.

You sit at the kitchen table, staring at the application form. What's the right move?

What do you decide?

  1. Enrol in the full program - go all in on

career growth.

→ **Go to Page 112**

2. Skip formal study and continue building experience in your current job.

→ **Go to Page 17**

3. Try a cheaper online micro-credential course first.

→ **Go to Page 56**

Build an Emergency Fund

You open a high-interest savings account and begin automating transfers each payday. You don't touch it, no matter how tempting. Within six months, you've saved $3,000. One day, your laptop dies unexpectedly. The repair quote is $700. You pay it upfront, no stress. Riley's impressed. You feel like the calm in the storm.

Points: +10

Lesson: An emergency fund gives you peace of mind. When life throws you a curveball, you don't need to panic or borrow.

→ **Go to Page 175**

Future-Focused

You contribute the full inheritance into your superannuation. The tax benefits are excellent, and your retirement balance jumps significantly.

You feel calmer, knowing your future is more secure. You and Riley start casually planning your "someday" retirement trips.

Points: +5

Lesson: Using windfalls for long-term gain helps secure your future. Superannuation offers excellent compounding and tax advantages over time.

→ **Go to Page 80**

Continue Expanding Your Stock Portfolio With More ETFs.

You and Riley decide to stick with what's worked so far: investing in a diversified range of ETFs. You both agree that your portfolio is already well-balanced and that you can continue adding more funds to increase your exposure to different markets.

Over time, the stock market fluctuates, but the ETFs continue to provide steady returns. You feel confident in your decision to maintain a diversified portfolio without taking on additional risk through real estate or cryptocurrency. As you approach retirement, you're happy with the consistent growth, and you see this investment strategy as both safe and effective for your long-term goals.

Points: +5

Lesson: Expanding a diversified portfolio of ETFs is a low-risk way to grow your wealth over time. While it may not provide the big wins of other asset classes, it's a stable and reliable choice for consistent returns.

→ **Go to Page 68**

The Starter Home

You buy the smaller place. The paint needs updating, and the bathroom's... fine. But the mortgage repayments are comfortable, and you still have savings left. You furnish it slowly, take pride in DIY improvements, and never feel overwhelmed. The financial breathing room means you can still travel, invest, and plan your future without the weight of debt.

Points: +10

Lesson: Buying a home within your means gives you flexibility and reduces financial stress. Property is a long-term investment, and starting with something manageable builds equity and stability.

→ **Go to Page 134**

Random Life Event: Market Dip - What Will You Do?

You're three months into your investment when it happens.

The market dips. Headlines scream *"Tech Stocks Plummet After Global Shake-Up!"* and your $500 investment drops to $465 in a single day. Your heart sinks.

Riley notices your anxiety. "You okay?"
"My shares dropped. I'm thinking of pulling out before it gets worse."

Riley pauses. "Isn't that the opposite of what you're supposed to do?"

You check your app for the fifth time that hour. The red numbers glare at you.

You now face a new decision:

1. Sell the investment before it drops further.
   → **Go to Page 18**
2. Hold your ground and wait it out.
   → **Go to Page 27**

Say No

You explain you've been saving hard for your future. Riley says they understand... but you feel the distance grow slightly. They figure it out by borrowing from their uncle instead, but it lingers. You wonder if it was the right call.

Points: -5

Lesson: Boundaries are important, but so is compassion. If you can help, consider doing so but not at the cost of your own financial security.

→ **Go to Page 106**

The Big Purchase - Your First Home

Age: 26

You and Riley have been saving hard. Between pay rises, budgeting wins, and the occasional windfall (if you played it right), your home deposit fund is looking strong. The dream is tangible now, and every little sacrifice feels purposeful. You create a vision board, filled with pictures of cozy living rooms, inviting kitchens, and a garden where you could eventually grow your own vegetables. It becomes a constant reminder of what you're working toward.

Weekends become dedicated to open houses and real estate browsing. You walk through properties, imagining where you'd put your furniture and how you'd make each space your own. There's a palpable excitement in the air, a sense of moving forward. You set a clear goal to buy within two years, calculating how much you need to save each month to make it happen.

Sticking to a strict budget is challenging. There are moments when you're tempted to dip into your savings for a quick getaway or an impromptu shopping spree. But Riley is a steadying influence, always bringing you back to the bigger picture. "We're so close," they remind you during one of your weaker moments. Their encouragement helps you stay on track, and before long, your account balance begins to look promising.

The progress fuels your motivation. Each dollar saved feels like a brick added to the foundation of your future home. The small sacrifices - cooking at home, skipping expensive outings, finding joy in simple pleasures - start to feel less like burdens and more like steps along the path to achieving something meaningful. You and Riley grow even closer, united by your shared dream and the discipline it takes to make it real.

You and Riley are filled with a mix of excitement and nerves as you begin exploring neighbourhoods, visiting open houses, and browsing real estate listings online. Every house you visit feels like a new possibility, like a blank canvas where you could create your future.

Some homes are charming but small, while others have the space you need but push your budget to its limits. The decision between a modest starter home and a larger, dreamier property becomes a recurring topic over morning coffee and late-night pillow talks.

You find yourselves weighing pros and cons: a smaller home means financial comfort and flexibility, while a bigger home offers space for growth and future opportunities.

You both imagine what life could look like in each home. In the smaller house, you picture cozy movie nights, the ease of lower mortgage payments, and the freedom to continue saving and investing. In the larger home, you envision hosting family gatherings, having space for a home office or a nursery, and building long-term equity. The choice isn't just about finances, it's about the life you want to build together.

When it comes time to make a decision, you feel the weight of the choice. It's a defining moment, not just in your financial journey but in your relationship as well. You and Riley promise to support each other no matter which path you choose, knowing that this is just one of many big decisions you'll face together.

- A **small, affordable home** within budget, in a decent area. Nothing fancy, but it's solid and manageable.

- A **larger, modern home** just outside your ideal area. It's $100,000 more than your budget-but your broker says you *could* get the loan if you stretch your mortgage repayments.

You and Riley debate for days. The bigger home would be a dream but the price tag comes with pressure. The smaller place is safer but feels a little underwhelming after everything you've imagined.

Time to decide:

1. Buy the affordable starter home within your budget.
   → **Go to Page 73**
2. Stretch the budget for the dream home, even if it means a bigger mortgage.
   → **Go to Page 99**

Random Life Event: Market Crash or Windfall

This year, the global market takes a hit. The sharemarket drops 15%, your portfolio drops $30,000, and headlines scream recession. Or, alternatively, your small business lands a $15,000 contract, giving you a sudden cash surplus.

Which scenario did you roll?

Flip a coin:

- Heads = Market Crash
  → **Go to Page 48**
- Tails = Business Windfall
  → **Go to Page 168**

Look into Life Insurance and Income Protection

After discussing the education fund, you and Riley agree that your family's financial security is just as important. You both decide to take out life insurance policies that will cover a significant amount in the event that one of you is no longer around. Additionally, you opt for income protection insurance to ensure that if either of you were to become sick or injured and unable to work, you'd still have an income to rely on.

A few years later, the unexpected happens. Riley becomes seriously ill and needs time off work for treatment. You're both grateful for the decision you made earlier, as the income protection ensures that your bills and expenses are covered during this tough period. Though it's not the best situation, knowing you've planned ahead brings you both a sense of relief and peace during a stressful time.

Points: +5

Lesson: Life insurance and income protection offer crucial financial security in case of illness, injury, or unforeseen events. They ensure that your family's well-being isn't jeopardized during tough times.

→ **Go to Page 97**

Invest It All

You convince yourself you'll "beat the system" by putting all $5,000 into ETFs. You skip the credit card payment this month and hope the market keeps rising.

At first, it feels smart. The market grows by 7% over a few months, but meanwhile, your credit card has quietly added $200 in interest. After a year, your investments are up... but your debt is barely budging.

Riley looks at the numbers. "Feels like we're treading water."

Points: –5

Lesson: You can't out-invest high-interest debt. The stock market averages 7–10% returns, but debt at 18–20% grows faster. Before you build wealth, make sure you're not leaking it through the back door.

→ **Go to Page 76**

Career Change or Business

You talk to your boss and negotiate a graceful exit. Then you launch your own consultancy business - working with clients in your field, but on your own terms. It's slow at first, but fulfilling. You work from home, set your hours, and never miss a school assembly.

You and Riley rework the budget, cut unnecessary expenses, and build a 6-month cash buffer for income fluctuations.

Some months are tight, but your mental health improves. You're happier and eventually, your income starts to rise again.

Points: +5

Lesson: A midlife pivot can improve life quality but it comes with risk. Always prepare financially before a big move: save a runway, reduce debts, and keep insurance active. Money matters less when you love what you do.

→ **Go to page 149**

Starting Adulthood

Age Range: Early 20s

Your twenties are a whirlwind of firsts. First full-time job. First car that's really yours (even if it's second-hand). Maybe even your first foray into renting a house. Life feels like it's moving fast, and you're finally making decisions on your own. But with freedom comes responsibility, especially when it comes to money.

For the first time, you're earning a steady income, and the possibilities seem endless. Nights out with friends, weekend road trips, or upgrading to the latest phone are now all within reach. But so are rent payments, car insurance, and all those little costs no one warned you about (like how expensive coffee can get when you grab one every morning). It's a stage of life where every financial decision feels like it could make or break your future.

Falling for Riley

Riley is someone who has quickly becomes one of the most important people in your life. Soon, the two of you are spending more and more time together. Riley's practical yet adventurous nature keeps you grounded but also pushes you to try new things. Whether it's a day trip to the beach or learning how to cook a decent meal together, Riley seems to make even the mundane feel fun. Before you know it, you're sharing dreams about traveling the world, buying your own place, and building a future together.

But those dreams also come with conversations about money. Riley suggests opening a joint savings account for a trip you're planning, but the idea makes you a little nervous. Sharing expenses feels like a big step - one you're not sure you're ready for just yet.

Friends, Freedom, and First Pay

Your friends are still a big part of your life, too. Sam is always suggesting spontaneous plans, like last-minute concert tickets or renting kayaks for a weekend adventure. Alex, on the other hand, is laser-focused on saving for their postgraduate studies, often reminding you of the importance of planning ahead.

Your first few pays feel like gold. You finally have the freedom to buy what you want without asking anyone's permission. But freedom has its challenges. One week, you splurge on a night out with friends, only to realise you've left yourself short for groceries.

Another time, you end up paying late fees on a utility bill because you forgot it was due.

And then there's the car. Your trusty old hand-me-down is on its last legs, coughing and spluttering every time you turn the ignition. The mechanic quotes a repair bill that's almost as much as the car is worth. Riley suggests looking into a used car together - something reliable that won't break down every other week. It's a tempting idea, but part of you wonders if you should just take the plunge and buy a new car instead.

The Balancing Act

This stage of life is a balancing act, one between saving and spending, independence and responsibility, enjoying the moment and planning for the future. There are days when you feel on top of the world, like when you get a raise at work or finally pay off a credit card balance. And then there are days when it feels like adulthood is one big math problem you forgot to study for.

But through it all, you're learning. About money, about priorities, about yourself. And as you navigate these decisions - big and small - you realise that every choice you make now shapes the life you'll live later.

→ **Go to Page 150**

Stay and Invest Aggressively

You double down on your investments. You boost your monthly ETF contributions, add to your super through salary sacrificing, and even buy into a managed fund. You rebalance your portfolio with a stronger tilt toward growth stocks and emerging markets.

You set a target: reach $500,000 in net assets by age 50. You track your progress monthly.

It's exciting but a little intense. Markets wobble, and your portfolio dips 8% one quarter. You breathe through the nerves and stick to the plan.

Points: +10

Lesson: Time is still on your side in your 40s. Growth-focused investing works, especially if you have 15–20 years until retirement. Just remember to rebalance periodically and plan for risk as you get closer to drawdown.

→ **Go to Page 149**

Big Celebration, Big Cost

The wedding is magical with fairy lights, laughter, teary toasts, and dancing under the stars. You have zero regrets about the day itself.

But when the photos arrive and the cake is long gone, so is your savings account.

You and Riley both agree: time to rebuild, fast.

Points: -5

Lesson: Some moments are priceless but expensive events can delay long-term goals. Be clear on what you're willing to trade off.

→ **Go to Page 64**

Withdraw smaller amounts.

You and Riley decide to take a more conservative approach. Rather than setting a specific withdrawal amount each year, you opt to withdraw smaller amounts each month, relying primarily on the income generated by your investments. This approach allows your principal to grow, giving you the flexibility to adjust your withdrawals if necessary.

At first, it feels like a smart choice, but over time, you realize it's limiting. When the stock market dips or interest rates fall, your income drops, making it harder to budget for larger expenses. While you live comfortably, the constant monitoring and uncertainty adds stress. The approach works for now, but you start to wonder if a more predictable withdrawal strategy would be better.

Points: +5

Lesson: Relying on investment income is sustainable for wealth preservation but can be limiting if income fluctuates. Balancing income with principal withdrawals ensures stability, even during market downturns.

→ **Go to Page 123**

Random Life Event: Health Wake-Up Call

At 54, you experience chest pain whilst out in the garden. It's not a heart attack, but it's a warning. The doctor says, "It's time to slow down. You've got to take care of yourself."

You now have to decide:

1. Cut your hours or retire early to prioritise health.
   → **Go to Page 133**
2. Ignore it and push on - you're so close to retirement.
   → **Go to Page 19**

Start a Side Hustle

You reduce your hours slightly and launch a small online business selling custom planners. At first, it's slow. A few sales here, some compliments there. Then, a social media post goes viral. Orders double. Riley helps pack boxes on weekends.

It's not enough to quit your job yet, but it's growing - and you're excited again. Plus, it gives you flexibility as you start preparing for parenthood.

Points: +10

Lesson: A side hustle can become a powerful second income stream or even a full-time gig. It brings flexibility and potential, but it requires time, discipline, and patience. Always start lean and reinvest profits wisely.

→ **Go to Page 129**

Invest Aggressively

You decide to prioritise growing your wealth. You increase your monthly investment contributions and diversify into property shares and international ETFs. You also set a five-year goal: reach $150,000 in your investment portfolio.

But you skip life insurance for now, thinking it can wait. One day, you catch the flu and it knocks you flat for three weeks. You're lucky it wasn't worse.

It's a reminder that health is unpredictable, no matter how smart your strategy.

Points: +5

Lesson: Wealth building is smart but not at the cost of *risk protection*. It's important to balance growth with safety nets. Consider a three-part plan: invest, insure, and save.

→ **Go to Page 176**

Deciding Not to Budget

You decide budgeting feels like too much effort right now. After all, money comes in, money goes out How complicated can it really be? You figure you'll just spend as you need and hope it all works out.

At first, everything seems fine. You treat yourself to a new hoodie, grab snacks after school with friends, and even cover your share of tickets for a group outing to the movies. But then, the unexpected happens: your phone charger dies (again!), and you need a replacement. No big deal, right? You stop by the store and grab one, but when you swipe your card, the screen flashes "Insufficient Funds."

The Domino Effect

Embarrassed, you step aside and check your bank balance on your phone. There's less than $5 left. You hadn't realised how quickly everything was adding up. The hoodie, the snacks, the movie ticket... it all seemed reasonable at the time. But now you're out of money, and your next pay isn't for another week.

The next few days are frustrating. You've already promised to join your friends for pizza on Friday, but you'll have to back out. On top of that, your bus pass needs reloading, and you're stuck asking your parents for help. They aren't thrilled about covering your fare and give you a lecture about managing your money better. Bethany thinks it is hysterical and takes every opportunity to remind you how dependent and bad with money you are.

Points: -10

Lesson: Without a budget, it's easy to lose track of where your money is going. Small purchases add up faster than you think, and when something unexpected happens - like needing a new charger - you're left scrambling. You tell yourself you'll try to be more careful next time, but deep down, you realize this might have been avoidable if you'd taken the time to plan.

→ **Go to Page 57**

** Mini Concept: Family Planning & Money **

Kids can cost around $140–$170 per week on average in some countries, and that doesn't include education or extra-curriculars. But financial planning isn't just about costs. It's about adjusting your lifestyle, protecting your income, and staying flexible.

Look into:

- **Paid parental leave options**
- **Childcare subsidies**
- **Health insurance** for dependents
- **Education savings plans** (like an investment fund or offset account)

→ **Go to Page 155**

Rent Out the Current Home

After some research, you and Riley decide renting out your home could supplement your retirement savings. The house is in a desirable area with high demand for rental properties, providing a steady income stream to complement your pension.

You find a small, affordable apartment nearby. The rental income from your home covers the apartment's cost, with extra left for savings or discretionary spending. You're glad you don't have to sell, and the rental income offsets your lifestyle costs, giving you flexibility.

However, being a landlord comes with challenges. You face tenant issues, maintenance, and occasional vacancies. While the extra income helps, the responsibility of managing the property is more than you anticipated.

Points: +5

Lesson: Renting out your property can provide a steady income stream, but it also requires ongoing management. If you're not prepared, it could become more of a burden than a benefit.

→ **Go to Page 187**

The Stretch

You go for the dream home. It's beautiful, open-plan, and even has a second bathroom. You move in and feel like you're living in a magazine. But within a few months, the reality kicks in - your repayments are tight. You have little left for savings or emergencies. When the hot water system breaks, you have to put it on a credit card.

You're house-rich but cash-poor. There's pride, but also pressure.

Points: –5

Lesson: Stretching your mortgage can lead to lifestyle strain. A bigger house isn't always a better decision if it prevents you from saving, investing, or handling unexpected costs.

→ **Go to Page 134**

Salary Sacrifice to Superannuation

You organise to salary sacrifice $300 a month into your superannuation. It's pre-tax, which means you barely notice the drop in take-home pay but your super balance starts growing faster. You watch your compound interest do its thing and feel quietly smug during tax time.

Points: +10

Lesson: Salary sacrificing lowers your taxable income and boosts retirement savings. Over 30+ years, this can make a huge difference. For example, $300/month invested at 7% annual growth for 35 years = $500,000+. Not bad for money you barely missed.

→ **Go to Page 125**

Retirement Begins - Living Off Your Wealth, Giving Back, and Leaving a Legacy

Age: 65

It's the first Monday you don't set an alarm. The house is quiet, the sun is already up, and Muffin 3.0 - older, slower, but still majestic - rubs against your leg in approval. Riley's making coffee, humming. No rush. No meetings. Just a slow start and a full day to do *whatever you want.*

You've made it. Retirement has begun.

You've built a healthy superannuation balance, your mortgage is long gone, and your investment portfolio is steady. You've downsized slightly with a smaller house and bigger garden, and you feel ready.

But after a few months of Netflix, coffee dates, and half-finished crossword puzzles, you start to feel... restless. Retirement isn't a pause. It's a new *stage* of life. So now comes a new question:

What kind of life do you want to live from here?

You reflect and consider how you want to spend your retirement:

1. Focus on enjoying life and ticking off your travel and lifestyle bucket list.
   → **Go to Page 165**
2. Dedicate time and resources to your family - helping children or grandchildren get ahead.
   → **Go to Page 143**
3. Find purpose through giving back, volunteering, or supporting causes close to your heart.
   → **Go to Page 157**

Split the Difference

You decide on balance. Half the refund goes to the credit card, the other half into your investment account. You feel a bit of everything - relief, progress, excitement.

Your debt still exists, but it's shrinking faster now. Your investments begin to grow. You watch both balances shift in the right direction.

Points: +5

Lesson: This is a decent middle-ground. You reduce your debt while building long-term wealth. But keep in mind - debt at high interest compounds against you faster than most investments grow. Still, if you stay consistent, this works too.

→ **Go to Page 76**

Debt vs. Investing

Age: 25

The Bonus Dilemma

It's tax time again, and you've just received a surprise $5,000 refund. You and Riley high-five in the kitchen, already tossing around ideas. New appliances? A short trip? Investing in more ETFs?

Then you open your banking app. Your credit card balance stares back at you: $4,000, racking up 18.99% interest.

Riley notices your silence. "That debt's been hanging around for a while," they say. "What if we knock it out?"

You nod. "Or... invest the refund and ride the market instead?"

You sit down that evening, tea in hand, laptop open. You have three options, and each will shape your financial path differently.

What will you do?

> **1.** Use the full refund to pay off the credit card debt.

→ **Go to Page 144**

2. Split it: $2,500 to debt, $2,500 to investments.

   → **Go to Page 103**

3. Invest the entire $5,000, keeping the debt in place.

   → **Go to Page 83**

Random Life Event: Raffle Winnings Reveal

Earlier, you won $100. Here's what happened:

If you spent it all: You had a great time but nothing to show for it.

Points: –5

If you saved it all: That $100 gained $10 in interest by now.
Points: +10

If you split it 50/50: You enjoyed yourself *and* grew your savings.

Points: +5

→ **Go to Page 164**

Making a Move

Age: 23

You and Riley decide to move in together. Rent, bills, groceries - it's a whole new financial world.

You each contribute to a joint account. Riley's still at university, so you take on a larger share for now.

But things are solid. You're building a life. You even talk about adopting a rescue kitten - Muffin 2.0.

Then the fridge breaks. You weren't ready.

Your Choice:

1. Pay for it on a credit card.
   → **Go to Page 118**

2. Dip into your emergency savings.
   → **Go to Page 181**

Delay the Repairs

You stare at the quote and flinch. "We can't afford this right now," you say. Riley agrees, reluctantly.

You decide to patch the roof yourself and save aggressively for the next six months to cover the repair. But with each rainstorm, the damage worsens. Eventually, mould appears in the ceiling, and a small patch of plaster collapses in the hallway.

When the time comes to get it fixed properly, the cost has grown to $9,800. You cover it with a combination of savings and a short-term loan, but it eats into your buffer - and your pride.

Points: -5

Lesson: Delaying necessary maintenance can make problems worse and more expensive. If you don't have the money, get creative (low-interest loans, partial repairs, or community grants). But avoid letting short-term savings goals sabotage long-term property value.

→ **Go to Page 119**

Over the following months, you settle into your work at the café. No incorrect orders and yes, you have had some coffee spills but only slight and only occasionally, and the customers were nice about it. With each pay, you see your account balance grow not just from deposits but also from interest. You're pleasantly surprised to see that money really can grow over time. This lesson sticks with you as you realise the power of saving and letting interest work for you.

Interest Explained.

Interest is basically the reward for saving money. There are two main types: straight-line interest (also called simple interest) and compound interest. The big difference? Straight-line interest is only calculated on the original amount of money (the principal), while compound interest is calculated on both the principal and any interest that's already been added. That means compound interest helps your money grow much faster.

Here's a simple example. Imagine you put $1,000 into a savings account with a 5% annual interest rate:

- **With straight-line interest**, you'd earn 5% on the $1,000 every year-so that's $50 each year. After 5 years, you'd have $1,250. Not bad, right?

- **With compound interest**, it gets more exciting. In the first year, you still earn $50, but in the second year, the interest is calculated on $1,050 (your original amount plus the first year's interest). Now you earn $52.50. By the end of 5 years, you'll have $1,276.28-more than $26 extra compared to straight-line interest. And that's just 5 years! Over 10, 20, or 30 years, the difference becomes huge. Plus, remember, that as you continue earning, you keep adding to the principal amount, which means your compound interest will continue to get bigger and bigger.

The cool thing about compound interest is that it rewards you for being patient. The longer you leave your money alone, the more it grows, not just from your original deposit but also from the interest that keeps adding to itself. Straight-line interest, on the other hand, is more predictable. It grows at the same steady rate every year, but it doesn't have that snowball effect.

Bottom line? If you're saving or investing for the long term, compound interest is your best friend. It's like putting your money to work so it earns more money, and then that money earns even more.

→ **Go to Page 44**

Go All In

You enrol. Classes are intense. You stay up late writing case studies and squeeze in lectures during your lunch break. It's tough but exhilarating.

You graduate in a year. Three months later, you're offered a new role with a $103,000 salary, remote work flexibility, and more creative control.

Points: +10

Lesson: Education can be one of the best long-term investments. If a course increases your earning potential *and* job satisfaction, the ROI often outweighs the initial cost, especially if you can pay upfront without debt.

→ **Go to Page 145**

Panic and Delay

The layoff hits you like a punch. "What are we going to do?" you mutter. Riley suggests looking at your budget, but you brush it off. "Let me breathe."

Days turn into weeks. You put off updating your resume. You sleep in, binge TV, and try not to think about it. Meanwhile, the bills keep coming. With no emergency fund in place, you start using your credit card for groceries, petrol, and bills.

Your limit is $3,000, and you hit it by the end of month two. Interest starts stacking up. You finally apply for the unemployment benefit and start looking for work, but now you're behind. Even when you land a job three months later, you're stuck chipping away at the debt with every pay.

Riley's supportive, but there's tension. "We should've been more prepared," they say gently.

Points: –10

Lesson: Without an emergency fund, even a short period of job loss can lead to debt and stress. Credit cards have high interest rates, often 17–20% or more. Using them for survival can quickly snowball. Preparation is key.

→ **Go to Page 52**

Random Life Event: Job Loss

Six months into your homeownership journey, your company downsizes - and your role is made redundant. Your manager is sympathetic. "It's not performance-related. We're just cutting costs."

You get a small redundancy payout but your income is gone, at least for now.

What do you do?

1. Dip into your emergency fund and focus on finding new work.

→ **Go to Page 147**

2. Panic, use credit cards to cover bills, and delay job hunting for a while.

→ **Go to Page 113**

Ask Family for Help

You swallow your pride and call your parents. It's uncomfortable - you haven't asked for money since university - but they don't hesitate. "We'll help," your mum says.

They transfer $3,000 into your account that day.

You promise to pay it back within six months. And you do. You cut back on takeaways, date nights, and unnecessary subscriptions. It's humbling, but manageable. You send a thank-you card with your final repayment, and a framed ultrasound picture of the baby.

Points: +5

Lesson: Family support can be a blessing but it should be a last resort, not a plan. Relying on others can strain relationships if expectations aren't clear. If you do borrow from family, treat it like a formal loan: agree on repayment terms and stick to them.

→ **Go to Page 170**

Support a Cause That Matters

You call your local library, where you and Riley have volunteered. "We'd like to donate $100,000 but with a plan."

You work with a charity adviser to establish a scholarship fund in both your names and Riley's mother - for underprivileged kids who love books, just like you did. The principal is invested, and the interest funds supplies, workshops, and even university tuition.

The first thank-you letter makes you cry.

Later that year, you speak at the library's reopening. "We don't take any of this with us," you say. "But we *can* leave something behind."

Points: +10

Lesson: Legacy giving isn't just for the wealthy. Even a single donation can change lives. Planned giving, through a will, trust, or scholarship, turns money into *impact*. Align your finances with your values for a legacy that lasts.

→ **Go to Page 139**

Swipe Now, Stress Later

You pull out the credit card. Easy fix. But interest piles up quickly. One card turns into two. You struggle to keep up.

Riley notices your stress. You talk and agree to build a proper emergency fund.

Points: -5

Lesson: Credit can be useful but debt grows fast if not managed. Emergencies are less stressful when you plan for them.

→ **Go to Page 104**

Diversifying Your Investment Portfolio

Age: 36

After years of successful stock market investing, you and Riley have built up a solid portfolio of ETFs, and you've watched your investments grow steadily over the past decade. However, lately, you've been hearing about the benefits of diversifying into real estate and other investments. With the economy unpredictable and stock market volatility increasing, you feel it's time to consider your options. You want to protect your wealth and ensure that you're not putting all your eggs in one basket.

After doing some research, you and Riley discuss the idea of branching out. Should you continue with your stock investments, or is it time to explore new avenues? You both agree that making a move now could provide both financial stability and future growth.

Choose what you want to do from the following options:

> 1. Begin investing in real estate or property trusts.

→ **Go to Page 177**

2. Continue expanding your stock portfolio with more ETFs.

   → **Go to Page 72**

3. Diversify into cryptocurrency and other digital assets.

   → **Go to Page 158**

Work to 65

You decide to stay the course. Your super continues to grow, and your investments compound quietly in the background. You pay off your mortgage at 55 and redirect that money into retirement contributions. You use the extra time to travel a little, fund your child's education, and even take up volunteering.

At 65, you will be able to retire debt-free, with a solid nest egg. You feel ready. You've worked hard, and now it's time to reap the rewards.

Points: +10

Lesson: Traditional retirement can be financially safe and stress-free if you plan well. You'll benefit from maximum superannuation growth, government pension access, and more time for your assets to grow. Just make sure to protect your health and maintain work-life balance.

→ **Go to Page 173**

Keep Investing in the Market

You continue contributing to your ETF portfolio each month. It grows steadily, though some months are rough. You learn about dividends - payments made from company profits - and start reinvesting them. Your portfolio becomes a second income stream. When markets dip, you don't panic. You've seen it before.

Points: +10

Lesson: Long-term investing is one of the most effective ways to build wealth. The average annual return of the global stock market over the past 100 years is around 7–10%, adjusted for inflation. Time in the market beats timing the market.

→ **Go to Page 125**

Downsizing to Free Up Cash for Retirement

As you and Riley settle into the rhythm of retirement, you begin to reflect on the years you've spent raising a family, managing a busy career, and maintaining a large family home. Your child is now grown, and the house, once full of energy and activity, now feels too big for just the two of you. The rooms are mostly empty, and the constant upkeep - cleaning, repairs, and managing the garden - feels more like a burden than a blessing.

Over dinner one night, Riley mentions how much more enjoyable life could be with less space to worry about. "We've got a solid retirement savings plan," she says, stirring her soup thoughtfully. "But what if we downsized? It could free up some cash for the next stage of our lives, and the house is worth more now than we ever imagined. Plus, we could invest that money to make our retirement even more secure."

You're both in agreement. The house has served you well, but it's time to think about how best to live the next chapter. With no mortgage left to pay, the house has become an asset you could use to bolster your financial independence. The thought of simplifying your life, cutting down on maintenance, and freeing up more funds for travel, hobbies, and family time is appealing. But there's still a lot to consider. Do you want to sell and move to a quieter area? Or perhaps you could rent out your current home and generate some passive income? Or, maybe staying put and renovating parts of the house would work best?

As the conversation continues, you think through the possibilities and the pros and cons of each option.

Choices:

1. Sell the house and move to a smaller property.

→ **Go to Page 166**

2. Rent out your current home.

→ **Go to Page 98**

3. Stay in the current house but renovate and downsize parts of it to make it more manageable.

→ **Go to Page 137**

** Mini Concept: Tax Efficiency **

You learn that how you structure your money matters:

- **Super** is tax-efficient but locked away until retirement.

- **Investments** are flexible but taxed on earnings (capital gains & dividends).

- **Savings** are accessible but earn lower interest.

Managing your tax efficiency can mean keeping more of what you earn.

→ **Go to Page 20**

Invest or Boost Super

Riley looks up from their screen. "We could invest this. Or add it to super?"

You nod. "Let's make it work for us."

You decide to split it strategically. Riley contributes their refund into super. You use yours to invest in your ETF portfolio. It's not flashy, but when you check your balances weeks later, you feel that satisfying sense of building something.

Riley's super gets a small tax refund boost thanks to the co-contribution from the government, and your portfolio grows slowly but steadily.

Points: +10

Lesson: Tax refunds are a bonus and treating them like income is a missed opportunity. Putting them into investments or super takes advantage of compound growth and tax efficiency. Every dollar you invest in your future has the power to multiply.

→ **Go to Page 135**

Begin Saving Aggressively For Your Child's Education Fund

You and Riley sit down with a financial advisor to talk about the best way to prepare for your child's future. The advisor explains the value of starting early and suggests putting money into an education savings plan that will grow over time with compound interest. With this plan in place, you both decide to set aside a certain amount of your monthly income, even though it feels like a stretch at first. You're both relieved to know that by investing early, the pressure of saving for college won't hit as hard when your child reaches their teenage years.

Over the years, the money in the fund grows steadily, and you feel secure knowing that you're investing in your child's future while also securing their educational opportunities. By the time your child is ready for school, you'll have a substantial sum saved up. You realize that while it requires sacrifices now, this move gives your child the best possible start in life, and you both feel proud of your decision.

Points: +10

Lesson: Starting early on saving for a child's education can relieve the financial burden later. Compound interest makes even small contributions grow substantially, so the earlier you begin, the better off your child will be when it's time for their education.

→ **Go to Page 97**

Planning for Family Growth

Age: 33

You and Riley have decided to start a family, but now you're realizing the financial implications of raising a child. Your current savings and investment strategies are important to consider, and you wonder how to adjust your finances for the future. How do you prepare for the new expenses that will arise from childcare, education, and general family growth?

Choices:

1. Begin saving aggressively for your child's education fund.
   → **Go to Page 127**

2. Look into life insurance and income protection for peace of mind.
   → **Go to Page 81**

3. Delay your plans for a child until you've saved more or paid off more debt.
   → **Go to Page 28**

Lend the Money

You lend Riley the money with a simple agreement. You'll work out repayments later. They're hugely grateful. The new (old) car runs well, and Riley lands a casual job to pay you back. Over six months, they repay every cent. You feel good because you've helped without losing anything long-term.

Points: +10

Lesson: Lending, when done with trust and clear expectations, can strengthen relationships. Just be sure both parties communicate and follow through.

→ **Go to Page 106**

Use Your Emergency Fund

You barely hesitate. You open your banking app, go straight to your emergency fund, and transfer the money. Seeing that balance dip, stings a little, but it's why you built it in the first place.

You cover the $2,800 bill immediately. No debt. No awkward phone calls. No stress.

Riley's resting in the hospital bed, baby monitor quietly beeping. "I'm glad we didn't have to worry about the money," they say.

You nod. "We planned for this."

A few weeks later, you start topping the fund back up with $200 a month, then more when you can. Peace of mind restored.

Points: +10

Lesson: An emergency fund is *not optional.* It's your financial seatbelt. It keeps you from spiralling into debt during life's unpredictable moments. Ideally, aim for 3–6 months of living expenses, stored separately in a high-interest savings account.

→ **Go to Page 170**

You Have A Win

That night, another friend of yours called Riley texts: **"Did you hear about the raffle at the library? I put your name down for a laugh... You won $100!"**

Another decision lands in your lap.

What will you do with your unexpected windfall?

1. Blow it all at the mall: you deserve it!
2. Save every cent: future you will be thankful.
3. Go half-half: save half and treat yourself (and Riley) with the other half

(Your points for this decision will be revealed at the end of this section.)

→ **Go to Page 109**

Prioritise Health and Slow Down

In the doctor's office you look at your test results. It's not dire but it's a red flag. "You're carrying too much stress," she says. "It's time to rethink your pace."

That night, you and Riley talk it through. It's not an easy decision, but it's a clear one: you scale back to three days a week. You've built enough of a financial buffer to do this. You even revisit your super contributions and reduce them slightly, giving yourself more cash flow to focus on wellness including healthy food, a personal trainer, and mindfulness sessions.

Your energy improves. Your sleep returns. You go hiking again. You laugh more.

Yes, your retirement fund grows a little more slowly but you gain something more important: *time*. You're alive, healthy, and present.

Points: +10

Lesson: Money is meaningless without health. As retirement nears, time and vitality become more precious than dollars. If your finances allow it, slowing down, even at the cost of growth, can *extend* both your lifespan and your quality of life.

→ **Go to Page 101**

** Mini Concept: Equity & Capital Growth **

Whichever house you bought, you've taken your first step onto the property ladder. Over time, your repayments help you build equity (the portion of the house you own), and if the market rises, your home could appreciate in value. But property isn't always a guaranteed win. Some markets stagnate or even fall. That's why buying smart (and within your means) is key.

You and Riley sit on your new couch, sipping tea and watching the sunset through the living room window of your new house. Riley turns to you and says, "We made the right choice." And deep down, you know they're right. The sacrifices, the careful budgeting, and the patience will all pay off. This is the first big step in securing your financial future, and it feels good.

→ **Go to Page 115**

New Life Goals - Kids, Career, and Changing Priorities

Age: 32

You're walking home from the shops with Riley, hands full of groceries and reusable bags, when they say, "So... I've been thinking. What if we started trying for a baby?"

You pause, smile, and feel your heart skip. It's not out of the blue - you've had quiet conversations in the past - but this time feels real.

Later that week, the two of you sit down to crunch numbers. There's the upfront costs - hospital, baby gear, time off work - and then the ongoing ones: nappies, childcare, food, clothes, education... It's a lot.

You also realise you're both at crossroads with your careers. Riley's been offered a leadership role, which would mean longer hours but more pay. Meanwhile, you've been daydreaming about starting a side hustle - a small creative business you could grow over time, perhaps even replace your 9–5 with.

You can't do everything. Something has to give.

You Face Three Big Decisions

Which direction will you take?

1. Take the leadership role and focus on maximising income for the growing family.
   → **Go to Page 167**
2. One of you steps back to part-time to prepare for family life, even if it slows financial progress.
   → **Go to Page 179**
3. You start your side hustle, aiming for flexibility and future independence.
   → **Go to Page 93**

Stay in the Current House but Renovate and Downsize Parts of It to Make It More Manageable

You decide to stay and renovate parts of the house to make it more manageable for retirement. You make key changes: turning an extra bedroom into a hobby office, converting the living room into a cozy space, and renovating the bathroom for better accessibility. With these adjustments, you've effectively downsized without leaving the house behind.

The renovations are a more affordable alternative to moving, and you feel comforted by staying in a space full of memories. The simplicity of updating your current home rather than relocating brings you peace, allowing you to enjoy your familiar, manageable environment.

Points: +5

Lesson: Renovating to downsize your current home allows you to keep the benefits of your space while making it more manageable. It saves money and stress compared to moving, but the renovations should align with your long-term needs and goals.

→ **Go to Page 187**

Combine All Finances

You merge everything - income, spending, savings - into one account. At first, it feels seamless. But then small things arise: Riley wants to buy concert tickets, you're saving for a new laptop. "Is it okay if I use *our* money?" they ask. You hadn't thought of that.

Points: –5

Lesson: Full financial merging can cause problems if spending habits differ. It's essential to maintain clear communication and some personal spending freedom.

→ **Go to Page 38**

Drawing Down on Your Retirement Savings

It's been a few months since you and Riley officially retired, and life is finally starting to feel like it should. The first few weeks were blissful: no alarm clocks, no deadlines, and plenty of time to relax. You've been enjoying long walks in the park, quiet mornings over coffee, and afternoons spent reading or gardening.

But now that the initial excitement of retirement has settled, you're beginning to wonder about the long-term picture. While it's been wonderful to not worry about work, you start to realize there's a big question hanging over your head: How much should you withdraw from your retirement savings each year?

Whilst working, you never had to think about how to draw down your funds. You simply saved, invested, and kept building your superannuation. But now, as your retirement years unfold, the reality of spending your savings rather than adding to them comes into focus.

You've heard of the 4% rule, a commonly recommended strategy where you withdraw 4% of your retirement savings annually to ensure your money lasts throughout your retirement. But you're not sure if this approach fits your lifestyle. You and

Riley have been talking about traveling more, maybe buying a motorhome for long trips, and indulging in hobbies you never had time for. The 4% rule seems conservative, and you're wondering if it's too restrictive for the lifestyle you envision.

You're ready to explore your options, but you want to make sure that you're not withdrawing too much too soon. After all, you've worked hard to get here, and you want your money to last as long as possible. But you also don't want to live like you're still in the grind of your job, saving every penny for a future that seems far away.

Choices:

1. Withdraw 4% per year to ensure your wealth lasts throughout retirement.
→ **Go to Page 160**

2. Withdraw a higher percentage for the first few years while you're still active, then reduce the withdrawal rate later.
→ **Go to Page 62**

3. Withdraw smaller amounts each month, relying on your investment income and keeping the principal untouched.
→ **Go to Page 91**

Early Retirement

You get serious. You cut spending, increase salary sacrifice, and take on a few side projects to boost income. You track your net worth obsessively, calculating when you can hit your "FIRE number" (Financial Independence, Retire Early).

At 58, you make the call. You scale back, sell your second car, and take long walks instead of long commutes. Riley joins you in early semi-retirement. You're not *rich*, but you're free. That's more valuable to you.

Points: +10

Lesson: Early retirement takes planning, discipline, and a lean lifestyle but it offers time freedom. FIRE followers often live by the 4% rule (withdraw 4% of your investments annually), so make sure you've saved at least 25x your annual expenses.

→ **Go to Page 173**

Ease Into It

You go part-time at 52, Riley follows at 54. The drop in income is offset by the reduced stress and increased time together. You still contribute to super, but you also start enjoying life more: weekday hikes, lazy brunches, slow living.

You will delay full retirement until 65, but those years in-between are the sweet spot with balance, freedom, and income.

Points: +10

Lesson: Phased retirement can offer the best of both worlds. You stay engaged, earn enough to cover expenses, and give your investments extra time to grow. Plus, it smooths the emotional transition out of the workforce.

→ **Go to Page 173**

Family First

You notice your adult child is struggling with housing. You offer to help with a deposit. Your grandchild needs braces so you pay for them. You babysit, cook dinners, help with school runs. You're the family anchor now.

You feel fulfilled knowing your money is helping the people you love *right now*.

Riley is on board, though you both sit down every year to make sure you're not giving away too much. You draw boundaries when needed, ensuring your own needs are still met.

Points: +10

Lesson: Financial support can build stronger families but it should be planned. You must balance generosity with sustainability. Consider giving *while living*, but set limits. Your financial independence allows your generosity to *continue* without risk.

→ **Go to Page 174**

Full Debt Payoff

You transfer the entire $5,000 to your credit card. Boom!Balance wiped. You let out a breath you didn't realise you'd been holding. Riley clinks their mug against yours. "That feels *really* good."

For the first time in years, you're free from credit card debt. You update your budget and reallocate the freed-up monthly repayments to savings and investments.

Points: +10

Lesson: Paying off high-interest debt is one of the best financial moves you can make. At 18.99%, that debt was costing you more than most investments could realistically earn. Clearing it gives you guaranteed returns *and* peace of mind.

→ **Go to Page 76**

Midlife Moves - Career Shifts, Wealth Strategy, and Thinking Ahead

Age: 42

You stare at the ceiling fan one night, unable to sleep.

Riley's beside you, softly snoring, and the house is quiet, except for the whirl of your thoughts. Work feels different now. You're good at your job, but the spark is gone. You've been thinking about making a change, something with more meaning or flexibility. Or maybe starting your own thing for real this time.

At the same time, your financial brain is ticking. You're earning more than you ever have, your mortgage is halfway done, and your super is growing but you wonder: *Is it enough? Are we on track for retirement?*

Riley's been thinking too. They bring it up over breakfast: "Should we talk to a financial adviser? We've done okay on our own, but maybe it's time to level up."

You both agree. It's time to be strategic.

You sit down one weekend and map out everything: assets, debts, super balances, investments, living costs, insurance, goals. Then you explore your options and realise you're at a crossroads.

Midlife brings both clarity and complexity. What's your next move?

1. Stay in your job but start investing more aggressively to boost future wealth.
   → **Go to Page 89**
2. Change careers or start your own business for more fulfilment and flexibility.
   → **Go to Page 84**
3. Work with a financial adviser to optimise your super, investments, and long-term plan.
   → **Go to Page 50**

Dip Into Emergency Fund and Take Action

You sit in silence for a minute after the call. Then Riley reaches across the table and squeezes your hand. "We'll figure this out."

After a deep breath, you pull up your savings account. Your emergency fund is sitting right where you left it - $6,000. You'd hoped to never touch it, but that's what it's for. You do some quick maths and figure out that with careful budgeting, it'll last you about three months if you cut back on spending.

That night, you revise your budget together, pausing streaming services, reducing takeaway, and putting a temporary hold on your investment contributions. You apply for Government assistance and update your resume.

Two weeks later, you land a few freelance gigs through a friend of a friend. It's not much, but it's something. You set a daily goal to apply for three jobs and make one connection on LinkedIn. The days are slow, but they don't feel wasted.

One month in, you score an interview. Then another. By the end of month two, you're offered a new role - same field, slightly lower pay, but a foot in the door.

You and Riley celebrate with a homemade dinner. You never went into debt. You used your safety net exactly the way it was meant to be used.

Points: +10

Lesson: An emergency fund is a financial safety net that helps you ride out tough times without spiralling into debt. Experts often recommend 3–6 months of essential expenses in a separate account. It's not exciting, but it's peace of mind.

↬ **Go to Page 52**

** Mini Concept: Superannuation Catch-Up **

You discover that your superannuation system allows for catch-up contributions if you haven't used your full concessional cap in past years. You can contribute extra and claim a tax deduction, which is perfect if you're earning more in midlife and want to boost your retirement balance.

→ **Go to Page 61**

First Full-Time Job, First Big Payday

Age: 21

Graduation's behind you. The awkward family photos, the cheap champagne, the feeling that something big is beginning - it's all still fresh in your mind.

You've landed your first full-time job at a media agency. It's a mix of admin, editing, and occasionally running for someone's forgotten lunch order, but it's solid. The pay is $55,000 a year. After tax, you're taking home around $3,600 a month. More money than you've ever seen. It hits your account the day before the weekend, and you can't stop staring at it.

Riley lands a graduate position too, and one night over a bowl of pasta on the couch, you both grin at each other. "We're real adults now," Riley says, raising their fork like a toast.

But with this new income comes a wave of decisions. The money feels like freedom... but also responsibility. Your inbox is now filled with words like superannuation, salary packaging, and income tax. You get an email offering to set up a meeting with a financial adviser through work. You ignore it. For now.

Your first adult money choice is simple, but powerful.

Your rent is $1,400 a month. After bills, groceries, and some modest spending, you reckon you could save at least $500 a month. Maybe more.

But the question is: what do you do with that spare cash?

Your choices:

1. Save all of it into a high-interest savings account and build an emergency fund.
   → **Go to Page 70**
2. Start investing in the stock market to grow your wealth faster.
   → **Go to Page 180**
3. Spend most of it - you've worked hard and want to enjoy life now.
   → **Go to page 30**

The Splurge

You both look at the $10,000 sitting in Riley's account and feel giddy. It's the most either of you has ever had at once. Within an hour, you're writing a wish list: a new TV, a plush couch, matching coffee mugs, and a trip up north to the Whitsundays. "We deserve this," Riley says. And you agree.

You take two weeks off work and head to a resort. The ocean is perfect. You drink cocktails by the pool, get massages, eat like royalty. Back home, you kit out the apartment in style. New everything.

By the end of the month, the money's gone.

At first, there's no regret. It was fun, memorable, exciting. But a few weeks later, you find yourself talking about saving for a house again, and it stings. That $10,000 could've made a huge difference. Now it's all on the "someday" list again.

Points: –10

Lesson: Spending windfalls can feel amazing short-term, but you often end up with nothing lasting. Had you invested it or put it toward your future, that $10,000 could have grown or helped build a foundation for bigger goals. Be cautious of lifestyle inflation when sudden money comes in.

→ **Go to Page 107**

Early Earner

You take the job offer. It feels good to earn a full-time wage, and you upgrade your wardrobe and move into a nicer place.

At first, it's great. But after a year, the job feels repetitive. You realise promotions are limited without qualifications. Riley, deep into their studies, seems to be planning something bigger.

Points: 0

Lesson: Earning early gives you a head start but without long-term planning, it might limit your growth. Consider how your current income aligns with your future goals.

→ **Go to Page 85**

Random Life Event: Unexpected Medical Expense

At 35 weeks pregnant, here are complications so you and Riley are rushed to hospital. Everything's okay in the end, but it requires extra scans, an extended stay, and follow-up care. Your insurance doesn't cover all of it. The bill is $2,800.

You have three options:

How do you pay for it?

1. Use your emergency fund.
   → **Go to Page 131**
2. Put it on a credit card to deal with later.
   → **Go to Page 53**
3. Ask your family for help covering the cost.
   → **Go to Page 116**

Keep Everything Separate

You continue splitting every bill and expense manually. It works... for a while. But over time, it gets tedious. "Did you pay the internet?" "I covered groceries last week, remember?" Tensions build. Eventually, you both realise this isn't working. You sit down and agree to change the system.

Points: –5

Lesson: Keeping finances separate works for some, but without structure, it creates friction. Clarity is key in shared financial commitments.

→ **Go to Page 38**

Giving Back

You start volunteering at a local charity and mentoring younger people in your industry. You even donate part of your super's earnings to causes that matter to you like animal rescue, climate advocacy, and rural education.

You feel connected. Energised. Retirement isn't a withdrawal, it's a reinvestment of your time and wisdom.

You also work with a financial adviser to set up a giving strategy that includes *leaving a legacy* in your will.

Points: +10

Lesson: Retirement is more than a number, it's a chance to *redefine purpose*. Giving back through your time, skills, or money creates impact beyond wealth. Legacy planning can include charitable trusts, foundations, or simply thoughtful giving with intent.

→ **Go to Page 174**

Diversify into Cryptocurrency & Other Digital Assets

After hearing about cryptocurrency from friends and online communities, you decide to dive into the digital asset world. You start with a modest investment in Bitcoin and Ethereum, hoping that the rapidly growing crypto market will provide big returns.

Initially, the market is volatile, and your investments see major fluctuations in value. While there are moments of excitement when the price shoots up, there are also days of panic when the market crashes. You and Riley both find it stressful but agree to keep the investments as part of your portfolio. Over time, you diversify into smaller altcoins, hoping to catch the next big breakout. While the journey is thrilling, you're also aware that this asset class is incredibly speculative, and you realize you could lose everything if the market crashes again.

Points: -5

Lesson: Cryptocurrency can offer high returns but is an extremely volatile and speculative investment. It's essential to only invest what you can afford to lose and balance these high-risk assets with more stable options.

→ **Go to Page 68**

Withdraw 4% Per Year

You decide to stick to the 4% rule, a well-regarded strategy for retirees. The thought of managing withdrawals carefully gives you peace of mind. With your superannuation and savings now providing a steady income, you calculate that this approach allows you to enjoy your lifestyle without the fear of running out of money.

This conservative method makes you feel secure. Each year, you check your portfolio's performance, and your withdrawal amount remains consistent. The stock market fluctuates, but because you've maintained your savings and limited your withdrawals, you don't feel the need to panic when the market dips. You adjust when necessary but always stay within the 4% range.

As the years go by, you and Riley travel more, spend time with family, and enjoy hobbies you put aside during your working years. You still budget carefully, but you've found that you can live comfortably without worrying about your financial future.

By sticking to the 4% rule, you have the reassurance that you're not taking on too much risk, and you can focus on what matters most: enjoying your retirement without stressing about your finances.

Points: +10

Lesson: The 4% rule is a proven method for ensuring your wealth lasts throughout retirement. It balances living well now with the financial security you need in the future. This approach offers peace of mind and minimizes the risk of running out of money too soon.

→ **Go to Page 123**

Preparing for Retirement - Freedom, Flexibility, and Final Moves

Age: 49

You're sitting on the back deck with Riley. The sun's going down, your teenager is yelling at a video game inside, and Muffin 2.0 is stretched out on a warm patch of concrete. You sip your tea, sigh, and say, "Can you believe we're almost fifty?"

Riley laughs. "Mentally? I'm 32. Physically? 84."

But the conversation turns real quickly. You've both been thinking about the same thing: retirement.

You open your laptop that night and check your superannuation. It's grown steadily with a healthy six-figure sum there now. Your investments are tracking well. The mortgage is down to its last few years. You feel... close.

But you also feel unsure. What does retirement *look* like? At 60? 65? Sooner?

Some of your friends are already talking about early retirement. Others have side hustles they want to grow. A couple are planning sea changes and tree changes. It gets you thinking.

Riley surprises you. "I think I want to retire early. Maybe part-time at first."

You blink. "We could actually do that?"

You review your options. What's your retirement strategy?

1. Work hard for another 10–15 years and retire at 65–67 with a comfortable cushion.
   → **Go to Page 121**
2. Aim for early retirement at 60 or earlier, even if it means making sacrifices now.
   → **Go to Page 141**
3. Shift to part-time work soon and ease into retirement slowly.
   → **Go to Page 142**

Fork in the Road

Age: 19

You've finished school, and university or full-time work looms. Riley's been accepted into a design course in the city, while you're still weighing up options: study, a job offer, or even a gap year.

Your savings are decent. Your budget has helped. But now the stakes are higher. Tuition costs. Rent. Commuting. Riley invites you to share a flat.

Mum offers advice: "Don't take on debt unless it helps your future."

Your options start to form:

Your Choice:

1. Enrol in university and take on a student loan.
   → **Go to Page 183**

2. Accept a full-time job offer and start earning immediately.
   → **Go to Page 154**

3. Take a gap year to travel and work part-time.
   → **Go to Page 35**

Bucket List Life

You and Riley draw up a list: Japan in cherry blossom season, hiking in New Zealand, cruising through the Mediterranean. You pull some funds from your investments and start booking.

You travel more in five years than you did in the previous twenty. You try new foods, meet new people, and create memories that feel more valuable than anything money could've bought.

You still keep an eye on your budget - you're not reckless - but you enjoy the fruits of your years of smart choices.

Points: +10

Lesson: Spending *with intention* in retirement is the reward for a lifetime of financial discipline. Don't hoard every dollar - experiences, relationships, and freedom are what retirement is *for*. Just make sure your drawdown rate is sustainable (typically 4% per year or less).

→ **Go to Page 174**

Sell the House and Move to a Smaller Property

After years in a bustling suburb, you both agree that a quieter, slower-paced lifestyle will be a welcome change. Moving to a smaller property would reduce your living expenses, freeing up more funds to enjoy retirement without financial stress. You start browsing potential locations, perhaps near the coast, or somewhere that's closer to the grandchildren.

You decide to sell your large house and move into a two-bedroom cottage with a lovely garden. The sale of the house gives you a tidy sum, which you invest wisely in safer, income-generating assets. The smaller home suits your needs perfectly: there's enough space for when the kids come to visit, and it's much easier to manage. Plus, you now have more cash on hand for travel and any unexpected expenses.

Points: +10

Lesson: Downsizing to a smaller property can reduce your living expenses, provide a sense of peace, and free up cash for other activities. It's an effective strategy for simplifying life while ensuring financial stability.

→ **Go to Page 187**

Take the Leadership Role

Riley accepts the role. The pay bump helps you top up savings, boost super, and build a solid financial cushion. But the hours are longer, and stress starts creeping in. Riley misses a few key moments - your friend's wedding, your favourite TV show together. You both feel it.

Still, you're financially strong. You can afford quality childcare, a reliable car, and even start saving for your future child's education.

Points: +10

Lesson: Maximising income is powerful during family years but it can come at a personal cost. If you take this route, pair it with intentional time together to keep relationships strong.

→ **Go to Page 129**

Business Windfall

It's just another Tuesday when the email lands in your inbox:

"Hi, love your work - can you quote us for a 3-month project?"

You do. You win the job. Just like that, your business earns an extra **$15,000**.

You and Riley celebrate with takeaway Thai and a shared grin. But instead of spending it, you pause. "Let's make this money *do* something," you say.

Together, you decide:

- $5,000 goes toward topping up your emergency fund
- $5,000 into your super via salary sacrifice (you'll claim the tax deduction)
- $5,000 into your investment portfolio

You also take 10% and treat yourselves to a weekend away. Guilt-free.

Points: +10

Lesson: Unexpected income is powerful when used intentionally. Most people treat windfalls as "fun money", which is fine, but it's also an opportunity.

Save, invest, and enjoy in balance.

Also, remember: *windfalls are rare. Your strategy is what matters most.*

→ **Go to Page 162**

The Next 10 Years - Growing a Family, Managing Risk, and Securing the Future

Age: 35

Your home is louder now. Messier. Happier. Toys underfoot, fridge covered in scribbles, laundry piles in strange places. You and Riley navigate parenthood together - half-blind with love and half-asleep from the 3am feeds.

Your cat, Muffin 2.0, now a seasoned observer, watches the chaos with veteran disdain.

The baby becomes a toddler. The toddler becomes a chatterbox. You blink, and suddenly you're packing a school lunch and wondering how you're already thinking about high school. Somewhere between daycare drop-offs and pay rises, you realise something:

You're not just building a life anymore. You're protecting one.

That night, while brushing your teeth, Riley says, "We probably need life insurance, huh?"

You nod slowly. "Yeah... and maybe income protection. And we should probably start saving for university."

You've got momentum now. You're earning more, your mortgage is ticking down, and your investments are growing but if something *unexpected* happened... would it all unravel?

It's time to make some protection decisions.

You sit down and map out your priorities. What's your next financial focus?

1. Take out life and income protection insurance - just in case something ever happens.
    → **Go to Page 36**
2. Start saving for your child's future education.
    → **Go to Page 54**
3. Focus on growing your investments - you're healthy and want to build wealth faster.
    → **Go to Page 94**

Invest for the Future

Riley brings you a glass of wine and says, "I want to do something meaningful with this money." You agree it's best used to help achieve a big goal, like a home deposit or a long-term investment.

You both agree to split it: $5,000 into your home savings account, and $5,000 into a long-term investment portfolio. Riley even sets up an automatic monthly contribution with a portion of their salary to keep it growing. "This way, the inheritance will keep working for us," they say.

It's not flashy, but it feels like a step forward. Every time you open the investment app and see it creeping upward, even just a little, you feel like you're building something real.

Points: +10

Lesson: Investing unexpected money toward long-term goals creates lasting value. A $10,000 investment, if left to grow at an average of 8% annually, could become $100,000 in 30 years. Windfalls are a rare chance to leap forward financially so don't waste them on fleeting pleasure.

→ **Go to Page 107**

** Mini Concept: The Retirement Toolkit **

At this stage, your financial plan includes:

- **Superannuation drawdown planning**
- **Age pension eligibility**
- **Investment withdrawal strategy**
- **Estate planning (wills, POAs, trusts)**
- **Healthcare coverage and aged care options**
- **Budgeting for 20–30 years of retirement**

→ **Go to Page 92**

** Mini Concept: Drawdown Strategy **

You learn how to manage your wealth in retirement:

- Withdraw *safely* (generally 4% or less of total assets per year)

- Mix income-generating assets (like dividends or rental income) with growth

- Use bucket strategies: keep 1–2 years of expenses in cash, mid-term in bonds, long-term in shares

- Reassess your needs and risk tolerance every year

→ **Go to Page 186**

** Mini Concept: Superannuation **

You start to hear about "super" from HR. It's your retirement fund where your employer puts in a percentage of your salary. You can add more if you want. It feels like a lifetime away, but guess what? The earlier you start, the more it grows. Why? Compound interest over 40 years is magic.

→ **Go to Page 74**

** Mini Concept: Financial Risk **

You learn there are three kinds of risk to manage:

1. **Market Risk** (investments go up and down)

2. **Personal Risk** (illness, injury, or death)

3. **Lifestyle Risk** (job loss, inflation, or under-saving)

Building a secure financial life means protecting against *all* three.

→ **Go to Page 60**

Begin Investing in Real Estate or Property Trusts.

You and Riley decide to take the plunge and invest in real estate. After consulting with a real estate advisor, you both identify a newly developed property not far from where you currently live. The property is in a growing neighbourhood with easy access to public transport and amenities, making it an attractive rental option. You take out a loan for the property, hire a property manager, and get the house rented out to tenants.

The rental income doesn't cover the entire mortgage, but you both hope that in the long term, the property's value will increase as the area continues to develop. With negative gearing, the tax advantages help you offset the short-term costs, and you feel optimistic about the property's potential for future gains. As the years pass, you see the value of your investment slowly appreciate, and although the cash flow isn't huge right now, the house becomes a significant asset that will provide you with long-term financial stability.

Points: +10

Lesson: Real estate offers potential long-term growth and passive income, though it requires patience. Negative gearing provides tax advantages, but it's important to be prepared for the short-term costs associated with property ownership.

→ **Go to Page 68**

One Goes Part-Time

You drop to part-time work. It's a stretch, but your emergency fund and solid habits keep you afloat. You have more time to prep for the baby, manage the household, and just *breathe*. Things are tighter, but less chaotic.

Some months are stressful. But when your baby arrives, you're both present. You're there for every giggle and every first step. The slower pace suits you.

Points: +5

Lesson: Less income means more financial discipline but for some, the trade-off is worth it. If you're choosing time over money, make sure your budget and safety net are strong.

→ **Go to Page 129**

Start Investing

You download a beginner investing app and put $500 into a diversified ETF (exchange-traded fund – an investment fund that tracks performance of a specific index, sector, or asset class, such as the NASDAQ, S&P 500, FTSE 100, or ASX 200, offering investors a diversified portfolio). It feels risky at first, but you're excited. You start tracking the market, learning the lingo, and watching your money fluctuate. Over a year, your investment grows to $550 - small, but steady. You're hooked.

Points: +10

Lesson: Investing wisely over time can build serious wealth but only if you stay consistent and don't try to "time the market."

→ **Go to Page 175**

Safety Net

You open your emergency account, sigh, and tap into it. The cost stings but there's no panic.

Riley high-fives you. "Smart move." You commit to topping it up again.

Points: +5

Lesson: Emergency funds are for exactly this. Planning ahead protects your future self.

→ **Go to Page 104**

One Last Big Adventure

Once you have had time to grieve, Riley says, "I want to see the Northern Lights."

That night, you book a business-class round-the-world trip: Norway, Japan, Patagonia, Morocco. You upgrade every room. You book a hot air balloon. You sip champagne at 30,000 feet and cry at the edge of a glacier.

You spend nearly all of the inheritance but the memories feel like gold.

When you return, you print a photo book. The final page reads: *Our memories are priceless.*

Points: +10

Lesson: Money is a tool. Used wisely, it buys not just things but experiences, meaning, and joy. If you've secured your financial foundation, it's okay to spend on moments that matter. Life is short. Make it vivid.

→ **Go to Page 139**

University Investment

You apply, get accepted, and take out a student loan. Orientation is nerve-wracking, but Riley's enthusiasm rubs off on you.

The classes are interesting, and you feel a growing sense of purpose. You keep a tight budget and take on casual tutoring gigs. Student life isn't glamorous, but you're building toward a future career.

Points: +5

Lesson: Education can be a smart investment but it's only worth it if it leads to better opportunities. The long-term payoff can outweigh the initial debt.

→ **Go to Page 85**

Blow the Refund on a Weekend Escape

Riley spins the laptop toward you. "Look. Spa retreat. Ocean views. Gourmet meals. We could leave *tomorrow*."

You hesitate - $2,100 isn't small change - but the pictures are stunning. You check the refund in your account. It's real. And it's tempting.

You book the weekend away. First-class train tickets. The ocean-facing room. Spa treatments. Three-course dinners. Champagne with breakfast. For two days, you live like royalty.

You return feeling refreshed... and slightly guilty. When your next gas bill is higher than expected and your credit card is close to the limit, the glow of the weekend fades a little. The refund is gone, and you're no better off financially.

Points: –10

Lesson: Windfalls are rare opportunities to make real progress and pay off debt, boost savings, or invest in your future. Splurging feels great temporarily, but the long-term benefit is often zero. A weekend fades. A stronger financial foundation lasts.

→ **Go to Page 135**

Half Now, Half Later

You and Riley sit down with mugs of tea and talk it through. "Let's enjoy it but not waste it," you suggest. You use $5,000 for a much-needed break and a few quality-of-life upgrades: a better mattress, a second-hand espresso machine, a couple of nice meals out. It feels good to indulge a little.

The other half goes straight into your shared savings account, earmarked for your future home.

You return from your trip refreshed, not just from the holiday, but from the knowledge that you didn't blow it all. A month later, when your car needs unexpected servicing, you don't even flinch. You've got a buffer now.

Points: +5

Lesson: Balance is key. Using some money to improve your lifestyle while still saving for the future builds both satisfaction and security. You avoid the guilt of spending *everything*, and the frustration of saving *nothing*. Smart decisions are rarely all-or-nothing.

→ **Go to Page 107**

Random Life Event: The Dreaded Call

One day, you receive a call. Riley's mother has passed away. You are both distraught at the loss - she was such a big part of both your lives, providing so much support, guidance and love - and to your surprise, she has left you an inheritance of $100,000.

Riley's eyes go wide. "That is so like Mum to do this. She should have spent more on herself instead of leaving it to us."

You have no urgent debts. You're comfortable. So, what will you do with this unexpected windfall?

What's your decision?

1. Invest it for your grandchildren's future.
   → **Go to Page 16**
2. Take one last extravagant overseas trip and enjoy every dollar.
   → **Go to Page 182**
3. Use it to support a cause or establish a scholarship.
   → **Go to Page 117**

Reflecting and Retiring

Retirement is here.

Riley retired a year earlier. You've paid off your mortgage, your super balance is solid, and your child has their own family and is living their own life, pursuing their own path.

You finally book that dream trip to Japan. You volunteer locally and spend time in the garden with Muffin 3.0, the cat you and Riley adopted a few years ago.

One afternoon, as you sit with a cup of tea, you look back on every decision you made. Not every one was perfect but together, they shaped a life of freedom, family, and financial confidence.

Final Points Tally

Add up all the points from your journey.

- 100+ points: You built a strong financial life and enjoyed the journey along the way.

- 70 - 100 points: A few bumps, but you've learned and grown. The future looks secure.

- Below 70 points: Some tough lessons - but it's never too late to rebuild. The next chapter is yours to write.

Thank you for playing Financial Fantasy. Your next real-life financial adventure starts now.

AFTERWORD

As you reach the end of Financial Fantasy, it's important to pause and reflect on the journey you've just taken. You've explored various paths, made key financial decisions, and learned the importance of understanding and mastering your finances. But the true value of this book lies not in the choices you made for the character, but in how you can apply those lessons to your own life.

Throughout the chapters, you've encountered real-world scenarios that highlight both the challenges and rewards of financial decision-making. You've seen firsthand how small choices can have a significant impact on your financial future, and you now have the tools to navigate these decisions with confidence and clarity.

The journey doesn't end here. Financial Fantasy is designed to empower you to take control of your financial destiny, but the real work starts as you apply these insights to your day-to-day life. Whether you're just starting out, planning for retirement, or working toward a financial goal, every step you take toward improving your financial literacy brings you closer to achieving the life you've always wanted.

Remember, financial literacy isn't a destination, it's a lifelong journey. There will be bumps along the way, and you may face setbacks. But each challenge is an opportunity to learn, grow, and get closer to your goals. Don't be afraid to make mistakes, because they are part of the process. The key is to keep learning, adjusting, and moving forward with purpose.

As you step into the future, armed with the knowledge you've gained, I encourage you to continue building on this foundation. Take control of your financial decisions, set meaningful goals, and make choices that align with your values. Most importantly, keep going - your financial freedom and empowerment are within your reach.

Thank you for joining me on this journey, and I wish you success and fulfillment in every financial decision you make moving forward. Your future is in your hands, and with the right tools, you can create the life you've always dreamed of.

Take action now - your financial adventure is just beginning.